BOOK OF BLACK HEROES

SCIENTISTS, HEALERS, AND INVENTORS

An Introduction for Young Readers

BY WADE HUDSON

To my father, Wade Hudson, Sr., and my mother,
Lurline Jones Hudson, and to those countless
Black heroes and heroines who paved the way for me.

Just Us Books, Inc.
356 Glenwood Avenue
East Orange, NJ 07017
www.justusbooks.com

Printed in Canada 10 9 8 7 6 5 4 3 2 1
First Edition
Library of Congress Cataloging in Publication Data is available.
ISBN: 0-94097-97-1 (paper)

"**Hero**: 1) one noted for feats
of courage or nobility of
purpose, especially one who
has risked or sacrificed his life.
2) A person prominent in
some event, field, period, or
cause by reason of special
achievements or contributions."

—*The American Heritage Dictionary*

About the Series

The *Book of Black Heroes* series is designed to introduce young readers to Black men and women who are heroes of their time. Some are from the past. Some are contemporary. But they all have overcome great obstacles to make significant contributions to our world.

Black people have made important inventions and discoveries, created great works of art, excelled in science, music, medicine and sports, and have been leaders of great nations and causes. But too often, the role that people of African descent have played in the development of civilization has been deliberately omitted from books. Centuries of racism and prejudice against Black people are the culprit. This omission has obviously had a profound effect on our society. It has helped to feed a feeling of superiority on the part of some Whites, and has result- ed in attitudes of inferiority among some Black Americans.

This series cannot correct gross injustices. It can, however, introduce some of the Black peo- ple who have made significant contributions to our world. Sharing this knowledge is another important step toward recognizing and appreciating the commonality of all the world's people.

Introduction

Book of Black Heroes: Scientists, Healers, and Inventors spotlights Black men and women who have achieved greatness in the fields of science, medicine and invention. Like many people of African descent involved in other disciplines, most of the women and men in this book have overcome difficult obstacles to reach a high level of achievement.

In the area of science, for example, racism has been a monumental roadblock to African American advancement. It has also prevented those African Americans who have overcome the odds from receiving the credit and recognition they deserve.

The aim of science is to find out how the world works. This is done through experiments, observation, and careful study. The knowledge obtained is put into a system so others can benefit from it and so it can be used to make life easier for everyone.

People have always been interested in understanding the world around them. Contrary to what many Europeans believed, this is and has been true of the people from the continent of Africa.

Author and educator Robert Hayden writes:

A book on the contributions of African Americans to American science should really begin in Africa. Contrary to popular belief, the African ancestors of today's African Americans had great control over the natural and physical world. That is, they could explain and predict the way things worked in their world. They knew how to use animal and plant materials for proper nourishment. They knew how to cure diseases and illnesses. They explored the uses of natural substances found in the earth. They knew how to use the natural energy sources of water, air, and fire."

Africans who came to this country in shackles brought that know-how with them. They used it to help build this country into a powerful nation. But because of racial discrimination and prejudice, most were robbed of the credit and recognition for their contributions. Since space exploration began in the 1950s, many African Americans have distinguished themselves in science. The lowering of racial barriers has provided them with opportunities previously unavailable. In addition, they are now being given rightful credit for their achievements. A number of these African-American scientists are included in this volume.

* Hayden, Robert. *Seven African American Scientists.* Twenty-First Century Books, 1992.

African Americans also have a heritage in medicine that reaches back to their African roots. For years, medical schools were closed to them. But some who were determined to render health care to their people learned their craft serving as helpers to White doctors. Others used the skills and knowledge that had been passed down from African tradition. Following the Civil War, a few medical schools opened their doors to African Americans. It was Black medical schools at institutions such as Howard University and Meharry College, however, that trained many African American doctors and nurses. Today, many of the most outstanding people in medicine are African Americans.

Before the Civil War, African-American inventors were not able to secure patents for their inventions. Many inventions were created by African Americans who toiled on plantations as slaves. Most of the slaves' inventions helped to industrialize a growing American economy. But slaves were considered to be the property of their masters, and according to the laws and practices of the time, all inventions slaves created belonged to their masters.

Free Blacks were also prohibited from registering and filing patents. Often, patents were secured in the name of a White person. After the Civil War, Blacks began to exercise the right to patent their inventions, but many still fell victim to unscrupulous business deals that robbed them of ownership and most monetary gains. Despite the obstacles, however, African Americans have been responsible for some of the most important inventions of the last century. Many are spotlighted in *Scientists, Healers, and Inventors*.

We are happy to have the opportunity to present so many Black achievers in this book. The research required has been a labor of love.

This volume is merely an introduction to some of the important Black men and women who have helped to shape the world in which we live. We could not include all of those who deserved to be selected. We hope the book will motivate others to learn more about the contributions of people of African descent. We all need to know about these important people. Black children, in particular, need to know about them, because these heroes and heroines can help them realize that they, too, can overcome obstacles and reach their goals.

—Wade Hudson

CONTENTS

SCIENTISTS

HEALERS

INVENTORS

SCIENTISTS

UNDERSTANDING OUR WORLD

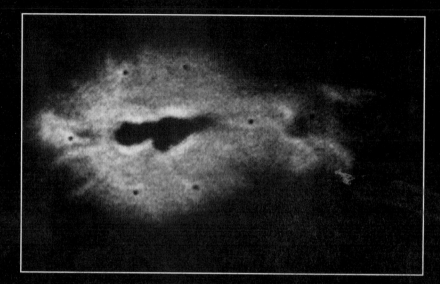

Inner core of so-called "symbolic star," *R Aquarii*,
photographed by NASA's Hubble Space Telescope,
October 4, 1990. *R Aquarii* is a distance of only
100 light years away from planet earth.

"You can't predict the future. That's what science is all about.
It's an activity of discovery. It's like peeling away the layers
of an onion. If I knew what was inside, there would be nothing
for me to do. A scientist carries out a series of investigations,
and you don't always know what is at the next layer."
— Shirley Ann Jackson, Ph.D

BANNEKER, BENJAMIN
ASTRONOMER

1731—1806
Birthplace: Ellicott, MD

B|enjamin Banneker was born free. His grandmother, who came to America as an indentured servant, worked and secured her freedom. After saving enough money, she purchased a plot of land and two male slaves. Later, she freed the two slaves and married one of them. Benjamin's father Robert was one of four children born to the couple.

Benjamin grew up on a 102-acre farm his father owned near Baltimore, Maryland. Benjamin's grandmother taught him to read. When he was old enough, his parents enrolled him in an integrated neighborhood school. Benjamin loved school, and he loved books.

When Benjamin left school to help on his father's farm, the world became his classroom. He studied the weather, animal life, the stars—everything he could. He read all the books that were available to him. By the time he was 20, Benjamin could answer the most difficult questions about mathematics, science, and philosophy.

In 1761, he carved a wooden clock by hand, using only two models—a pocket watch and an old picture of a clock. It is said that the clock kept nearly perfect time for 50 years.

A solar eclipse happens when the moon passes between the sun and the earth, casting a shadow on the earth. As an astronomer, Benjamin correctly predicted that a solar eclipse would occur in 1789.

A few years later, Benjamin published an almanac that became immediately successful. Farmers used it to help them decide when to plant their crops. Benjamin's almanac was more accurate than the almanac published by Benjamin Franklin.

Benjamin Banneker also helped survey the site for Washington, D.C., the nation's capital. When Major Pierre-Charles L'Enfant, the man President George Washington selected to design the new capital, resigned and went to France, Benjamin and the other surveyors continued the work, and the nation's capital was built.

Although Benjamin had never been a slave, he spoke out against the system that held his people in bondage. The young man who studied the stars made many important contributions to our young country.

BLUFORD JR., GUION
AEROSPACE ENGINEER

1942—
Birthplace: Philadelphia, PA

During the early morning hours of August 30, 1983, the space shuttle *Challenger* blasted off for its third flight. Among the five-man crew was Lieutenant Colonel Guion S. Bluford, Jr.

For Guy, as he was often called, this trip into space was a dream come true. As a child growing up in Philadelphia, Pennsylvania, he would close his eyes and visualize himself in a spaceship headed into the solar system. Guy built model airplanes and studied their movement. He spent countless hours trying to understand the dynamics of flight. During the 1950s both the United States and the Soviet Union were beginning their space programs. On October 4, 1957, the Soviet Union launched *Sputnik 1*, the first artificial satellite, into space. Guy was 14 years old. Then, on January 31, 1958, the United States launched its first satellite, *Explorer 1*. The space age had begun, and Guy, like so many others, was caught up in the excitement.

In 1960 Guy entered Pennsylvania State University to study aerospace engineering. He completed his four years of study in 1964, earning distinguished Air Force ROTC honors. After graduation he attended pilot training at Williams Air Force Base in Arizona where he received his pilot wings. During the Vietnam War, Guy was assigned to the 557th Tactical Fighter Squadron in Vietnam, where he flew 144 combat missions. Guy's years as a fighter pilot were challenging, but he never lost his desire to explore space.

In January 1978, Guy, along with 34 others, was selected as a candidate for the astronaut program. Among the others were Sally K. Ride, who became the first woman in space, and Ronald McNair and Fred Gregory, two other African Americans. Now Guy had a chance to become an astronaut and fly in space. After successfully completing the rigorous NASA training program, Guy was chosen to be an astronaut in August 1979. In April 1982 NASA announced that he had been selected for the space shuttle mission scheduled to launch in the summer of 1983. On August 31, Guy Bluford, Jr. became the first African American to fly in space. He has since been on two other space missions, one in 1985 and another in 1991. Guy now works for the astronaut office helping to prepare others for space missions.

CARRUTHERS, GEORGE E.
AERONAUTICAL ENGINEER

1939—

Birthplace: Cincinnati, OH

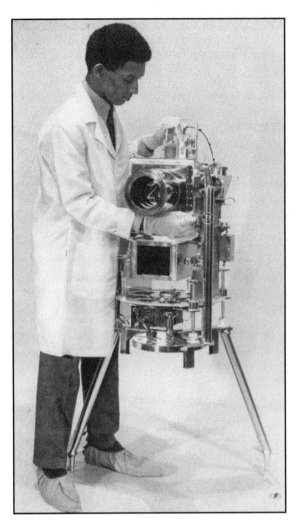

S|pace exploration. The mere mention of those two words has stirred the imagination of many youngsters fascinated by the stars, planets, and other celestial bodies. One such youngster was George E. Carruthers.

George was born in Cincinnati, Ohio in 1939 and later moved to Chicago, Illinois. Even as a young child, living with his parents in the housing projects of Chicago's South Side, he was interested in outer space. He enjoyed watching the sky, and when he was 10, he built his first working telescope.

After reading several books on astronomy given to him by his father, astronomy became George's hobby. He spent much of his free time at the local planetarium. Although George was seldom encouraged by the scientists he met at the planetarium, he was determined to study hard and achieve his goal of becoming a scientist. He had read about Benjamin Banneker, the 18th century Black astronomer and scientist who helped layout the city of Washington, D.C. Benjamin Banneker became a role model for George.

George's hard work in school paid off when he received a scholarship to the University of Illinois. In 1961, he graduated with honors, and a bachelor's degree in aeronautical engineering. He then earned a master's degree in nuclear engineering and a doctorate degree in aeronautical engineering.

George began working for the Naval Research Laboratory in Washington, D.C. There he worked on a design for an electromagnetic imaging device. George invented the camera-spectrograph in 1972, when he was 32 years old. It became the earth's first moon-based observatory when it was placed on the moon as a part of the Apollo 16 project. George received a patent for his invention, and William Conway, a naval researcher, adapted the camera for the lunar mission. The device was used to gather photographic images of the earth's upper atmosphere. The camera-spectrograph was later adapted for use on Skylab 4, which tracked the progress of the comet *Kohoutek* in 1974.

George Carruthers continues to work on experiments for missions in space. He also encourages African–American teachers to get involved in science and technology.

CARVER, GEORGE W.

BOTANIST

1864—1943
Birthplace: Diamond Grove, MO

When George Washington Carver died on January 5, 1943, he was one of America's most honored scientists. From his modest laboratory at Tuskegee Institute in Alabama, George rescued a dying agricultural economy in the South by helping to institute methods to replenish the soil, thereby increasing crop production. He discovered hundreds of products that could be made from the peanut, the sweet potato, and the pecan, and became an authority on plant diseases. He was also a role model for many African Americans who were struggling to lift themselves out of poverty through education.

Born on a plantation in Diamond Grove, Missouri in 1860, George was still a baby when he, his mother, and sister were kidnapped by a band of night raiders. The plantation owner got George back in exchange for a racehorse, but George's mother and sister were not recovered and George never saw them again.

As a child, George spent most of his time in the woods, studying flowers, insects, birds, and animals. He was 20 years old when he finished high school and had overcome many hardships to do so. Because of his excellent academic record, a university in Kansas offered him a scholarship, but when the president saw that he was Black, he turned George away. Finally, Simpson College in Iowa accepted George as the school's first Black student. A few years later, George transferred and became the first Black student to attend the Iowa State College of Agriculture and Mechanical Arts.

In 1894, a proud George Washington Carver was rewarded for his hard work and determination when he received his bachelor of science degree from Iowa State College. He was then offered a job there teaching botany and agriculture and overseeing the greenhouse. Two years later George earned his master's degree in agriculture.

In 1896, Booker T. Washington, the Black leader and founder of Tuskegee Institute, a leading college for African Americans, asked George to head the school's agriculture department. George accepted. He remained there for 47 years, earning honors for himself and for the school he loved so much.

COBB, JEWEL PLUMMER

CELL BIOLOGIST

1924—
Birthplace: Chicago, IL

Jewel was born into a family of doctors and Ph.D.s. Her father had a medical practice in Chicago, where he cared for African-American patients. Following in her father's footsteps, Jewel became a third generation doctor. Her son, a radiologist, became the fourth.

Despite being surrounded by doctors and science all her life, it wasn't until Jewel was a sophomore in high school that she looked through a microscope in a laboratory and decided that biology was for her. After graduating from high school, she attended the University of Michigan, but she left because Black students were not allowed to live in the dormitories. This was in 1941. She transferred to Talladega, a Black college, and graduated in 1944.

After receiving her doctorate degree in cell biology from New York University in 1950, Jewel did cancer research. She wrote over 36 papers and performed extensive studies of cell biology with the hope of finding some clue to the cure for cancer. Jewel became very well known as a prominent cancer researcher.

During her career, Jewel has held many faculty and administrative positions at various universities, including deanships at Connecticut College and Douglass College at Rutgers University in New Jersey. All the while, she continued to conduct research. In 1981, she was named president of California State University at Fullerton, which at the time had a student enrollment of 22,000. With that appointment, Jewel became one of the few African-American women to head a college or university.

Jewel is currently serving as President Emeritus at California State, Fullerton, and as Trustee Professor. But despite her success as an administrator and educator, Jewel still considers herself, first and foremost, a biologist.

Jewel is worried, however, that more African-American students are not going into science. "When I see more Black students in the laboratories than I see on the football field," she has said, "then I'll be happy."

COLE, JOHNNETTA

ANTHROPOLOGIST

1936—
Birthplace: Jacksonville, FL

An anthropology course that 17-year-old Johnnetta Cole took to fulfill a liberal arts require-ment while attending Oberlin College changed her career goals permanently. After trans-ferring from Fisk University, Johnnetta focused on pursuing a career in medicine. But the pro-fessor of her anthropology class made the study of humans seem exciting and challenging. Johnnetta changed her major to anthropology and received her degree from Oberlin in 1957. She went on to graduate school at Northwestern University where she studied under noted anthropologists Melville Herscovits and Paul J. Bohannan. Later, Johnnetta went to Africa to conduct anthropological research. She used the data she accumulated to write her Ph.D. disser-tation. She received her doctorate from Northwestern in 1967.

Johnnetta was hired as an assistant professor of anthropology at Washington State University, where she was instrumental in establishing the school's Black Studies Program. In 1970, she was offered a tenured position at the University of Massachusetts. There she spent 13 years teaching courses in anthropology and Afro-American studies.

In 1986, Johnnetta published *All-American Women: Lives that Divide, Ties That Bind*, a book that examines the issues of race, class, gender, and ethnicity.

That same year Spelman College, a historically Black college for women and one of the country's premier institutions of higher learning, started a search for a new president. Finding a Black woman to fill the position was a top priority. In 1987, Johnnetta was named to the top post, becoming the first Black woman in the school's history to hold this important position. Johnnetta was instrumental in increasing contributions to the endowment of Spelman. On the day Johnnetta was inaugurated, entertainer Bill Cosby and his wife Camille presented $20 mil-lion to the college.

In 1993, Johnnetta published her second book *Conversations: Straight Talk with America's Sister President*. In it, she targets a multiplicity of audiences with her message of equality. Johnnetta Cole has been a role model for many young Black women. Her influence, however, reaches across color and gender lines. In 2002 she came out of retirement to accept leadership of Bennett College in South Carolina, the only other Black woman's college in the United States.

COLEMAN, BESSIE

AVIATOR

1893—1926
Birthplace: Atlanta, TX

B essie Coleman was the first Black woman ever to fly an airplane. She was also the first African American to earn an international pilot's license. But as a youngster growing up in Waxahachie, Texas, very few people would have thought Bessie would become such an important person.

Born in Atlanta, Texas, in 1892, she was one of 13 brothers and sisters. When she was two years old her family moved to a small farm near the town of Waxahachie, Texas, about 30 miles south of Dallas.

When Bessie was nine, her father returned to his home state of Oklahoma to seek better employment. Bessie's mother Susan remained in Texas with the children where she took in laundry and picked cotton to support the family. Bessie was responsible for looking after her younger brothers and sisters.

Bessie was an eager student who excelled in mathematics. After completing the eighth grade, young Bessie found a job as a laundress. She wanted to save enough money to continue her education. In 1910, she enrolled in an Oklahoma preparatory school, but her money ran out and she was forced to return home. Finally, Bessie tired of her hometown. She decided to join her brother Walter in Chicago. There, Bessie completed a course in manicuring and began a career as a manicurist. Within a short time she had earned a reputation as the "best and fastest manicurist" in Chicago. But Bessie had something quite different on her mind. She wanted to fly airplanes.

The mere thought of flying excited Bessie, but during the early 1920s women pilots were rare and Black women pilots were unheard of. But that didn't stop Bessie. She applied to a number of aviation schools, but every one rejected her. A friend suggested she learn French and apply to a school in France. Bessie did and she was accepted.

In 1921, Bessie received her flying license after completing seven months of instruction and passing a tough qualifying examination. The determined Bessie was now the first Black female pilot ever. From 1922 to 1926 Bessie performed flying exhibitions at air shows where she executed daredevil maneuvers. She gave lectures on aviation, too. She wanted to inspire young African Americans to enter the field of aviation. Tragically, the career that Bessie loved led to her death. In April 20, 1926, during a practice flight, the aviator whom many called the world's greatest woman flyer was killed when she was thrown from her plane.

GOURDINE, MEREDITH
ENGINEER & PHYSICIST

1929—1998
Birthplace: Livingston, NJ

Meredith Gourdine is an example that brains and athletic prowess can coexist in the same person. An outstanding student in high school and college, Meredith won a silver medal in the long jump at the 1952 Olympics in Helsinski, Finland. His athletic exploits in track earned him the nickname "Flash." It was in science, however, that Meredith really shone.

Meredith was born in Livingston, New Jersey, but grew up in New York City. He attended a Catholic elementary school in Harlem and was accepted at Brooklyn Tech, a school for exceptional science students. Young Meredith excelled at Brooklyn Tech, and earned a scholarship to Cornell University. At Cornell, he majored in engineering physics. In 1960, he was awarded a doctorate in engineering science by the California Institute of Technology. After working two years at the Curtiss-Wright Corporation as chief scientist, he started his own company.

In 1969, Meredith developed an electrogas dynamic (EGD) generator as an alternative to water powered generators. The small generator produced a lot of power by harnessing large forces in a small space. From 1969 to 1971, Meredith was awarded 15 patents in electrogas dynamics.

The EGD generator has had practical uses in food refrigeration, producing heat and light in residences, and in burning gas more efficiently. Other inventions credited to Meredith include an exhaust purifying device for automobiles, devices for measuring air pollution, and generators for power stations.

Meredith lost his eyesight because of diabetes. But Flash didn't let that stop him. He continued to do research in electrogas dynamics, trying to find ways to make life a little better for humankind.

HALL, LLOYD AUGUSTUS
CHEMIST

1894—1971
Birthplace: Elgin, IL

During his long career, Lloyd Augustus Hall was granted more than 100 patents in the United States and abroad. His knowledge and innovations in food chemistry earned him numerous honors, appointments and seats on the boards of prominent organizations.

Lloyd was born in 1894 in Elgin, Illinois. As was the case with most scientists and inventors, Lloyd was an excellent student. His primary interest was chemistry. Elgin was the only African-American male student in his high school. There were four African-American female students. He graduated among the top ten in his class and received a scholarship to Northwestern University. In 1916, Lloyd earned a degree in pharmaceutical chemistry. He went on to earn graduate degrees from the University of Chicago and the University of Illinois.

Lloyd applied for a job with Western Electric. He had impressed a personnel officer during a telephone interview. But when he went to the office in person, the personnel officer, seeing Lloyd was African American, told the energetic young man, "We don't take niggers." Although he was hurt by the insult, Lloyd was still determined. He landed a job as a chemist with the Chicago Department of Health. Later, he was promoted to senior chemist. In the early 1920s, while working for Boyer Chemical Laboratories, Lloyd began to focus on food chemistry, particularly with the problem of preserving meat. At that time, meat often spoiled quickly. When Lloyd went to work for a chemical lab owned by a former college classmate, he began to make contributions to the area of food preservation. He developed a new meat preserving process, created sterilization techniques for foods and spices, and even patented a process that reduced the time needed to cure bacon.

Lloyd Augustus Hall helped to revolutionize the processing and preserving of meats and produce. Not only did he help food companies save a lot of money, he also helped to make the food we eat healthier and tastier.

JACKSON, SHIRLEY ANN
PHYSICIST

1946—
Birthplace: Washington, D.C.

In 1964 Shirley Ann Jackson was one of only 15 African-American students to enroll at Massachusetts Institute of Technology (M.I.T.), one of the country's foremost institutions of higher learning. In the beginning, college life was difficult for her. White students avoided her. She studied long hours alone. During her second semester, however, she was chosen to be a laboratory assistant because of her excellence in the classroom. Then students sought her as a tutor and study mate. Shirley had been taught well at all-Black Roosevelt High School in Washington, D.C., where she graduated in 1964 as valedictorian of her class. Her teachers and her parents instilled in her self-confidence as well as a desire to excel. Those virtues served her well at M.I.T. and in her chosen profession.

After Shirley graduated from M.I.T., she received scholarship offers for graduate study from Harvard University, Brown University, and the University of Chicago. She chose to remain at M.I.T. because her advisor would be Dr. James Young, the institute's first permanent African-American physics professor. At age 26, Shirley received her doctorate degree from M.I.T. She was the first African-American woman to earn a doctorate in physics.

Shirley worked at several laboratories following graduation, including the Fermi National Accelerator Laboratory in Illinois, the European Center for Nuclear Research, and Bell Laboratories in New Jersey. At Bell Labs Shirley did advanced communication systems research. Her main area of concentration was semiconductors, which are used to make solid-state electronic components.

Shirley contributed to many scientific breakthroughs while at Bell Labs. Some of the most gifted African-American physicists also worked at Bell, including Earl Shaw, the first African American hired by the company to do research, Roosevelt People, Kenneth Evans, and Walter P. Lowe. Later, Shirley was appointed professor of physics at Rutgers University in New Jersey. In 1995, she was appointed chairperson of the United States Nuclear Regulatory Commission, which is responsible for protecting public health and safety in the nuclear age. In 1998, she was named president of Rensselaer Polytechnic Institute.

JEMISON, MAE C.

ASTRONAUT

1956—
Birthplace: Decatur, AL

I In August 1987, Dr. Mae Jemison was sitting at her desk at a hospital in Los Angeles, California. She was between patients, taking care of some paperwork, when the telephone rang. It was a representative of the National Aeronautics and Space Administration (NASA). The young physician was told she had been chosen as an astronaut candidate. She could become the first African-American woman to travel in space.

This was just the latest in a series of notable accomplishments by the multi-talented Mae Jemison. Born in Alabama but raised in Chicago, Illinois, Mae received her bachelor of science degree in chemical engineering and a bachelor of arts degree in African and Afro-American Studies simultaneously from Stanford University. From there she enrolled in Cornell University Medical College where she became very active in student and community-based groups. She also maintained an interest in Third World countries. Mae traveled to Cuba, Kenya, and Thailand to work and continue her medical training.

After graduating from medical school, Mae joined the Peace Corps and worked in Africa supervising health-care programs for Peace Corps personnel. Upon her return, she worked as a general practitioner in Los Angeles. She then applied for admission to the astronaut program.

Three months after Mae first applied to NASA, the *Challenger* disaster occurred, taking the lives of seven astronauts, including that of an African American, Ronald McNair. But the incident did not deter Mae. She simply reapplied when the selection process was reopened. A year later, she was notified that she had been chosen from nearly 2,000 applicants as one of the 15 members of NASA's 1987 astronaut training program.

Mae completed a one-year training and evaluation program in August 1988. In August 1992, Mae traveled into space on *Space Lab J*, becoming the first woman of color to do so. This mission was a cooperative venture between the United States and Japan and focused on research in life sciences and material development. Mae is now a much sought-after speaker and consultant.

JULIAN, PERCY LAVON
CHEMIST

1899—1975
Birthplace: Montgomery, AL

Percy Lavon Julian was an internationally acclaimed scientist who was granted more than 130 patents during his career. Percy specialized in synthesizing innovative drugs and industrial chemicals from natural products such as soybeans and potatoes. His most notable accomplishments included finding a way to produce cortisone, which is used in treating rheumatoid arthritis, from soybean oil; synthesizing physostigmine, the drug used to treat glaucoma; and creating substitutes for male and female hormones. These hormone substitutes have been used to treat cancer, protect unborn babies, and to prolong male virility.

Julian grew up in the South around the turn of the century, when discrimination was rampant. Schools were segregated, and those established for African Americans were often housed in dilapidated buildings and had inadequate supplies and materials. Black youngsters were only required to complete the sixth grade. But Julian's mother and father wanted more for their son. They enrolled him in a private school for Blacks located in Montgomery, Alabama. Julian graduated in 1916 and then applied to DePauw University in Greencastle, Indiana where he was admitted as a "sub-freshman." He was required to take high school courses along with his normal college work because the university said his high school education was inadequate.

But Julian worked hard and graduated as DePauw's top chemistry student. He did not receive an offer to attend graduate school as his fellow White students did, so he accepted a position teaching chemistry at historically Black Fisk University in Nashville, Tennessee. In 1922 he was awarded a fellowship to Harvard where he received a master's degree. Later he was appointed associate professor and director of the chemistry department at Howard University, another historically Black university. In 1931, Julian earned a doctorate degree in organic chemistry at the University of Vienna, Austria, and returned to Howard as a full professor, where he began to conduct research with the soybean. Then he became chief chemist and director of research at the Glidden Company, a manufacturer of paints. Later he established his own research company, which he sold for $2.3 million. The NAACP recognized the outstanding contributions of this great chemist when it awarded him the prestigious Spingarn Medal in 1947.

JUST, ERNEST EVERETTE
CELL BIOLOGIST

1883—1941
Birthplace: Charleston, SC

Sixteen year old Ernest Just arrived in Meriden, New Hampshire excited and anxious. He had left his home in Charleston, South Carolina a few months earlier determined to enter Kimball Academy, a boys' prep school well known for its college preparatory program. Several months of work in New York had earned Ernest enough money to enter Kimball.

Ernest grew up in Charleston, South Carolina. His father, a dock worker, died when he was four years old. His mother taught school and was responsible for most of Ernest's early education. Ernest was an energetic and curious youngster who enjoyed playing outdoors and studying plants and insects. He wanted to be a teacher like his mother.

Ernest took advantage of his opportunity at Kimball. He graduated with honors, and in 1903, entered Dartmouth College in New Hampshire. While taking a biology course, he discovered the excitement and intellectual stimulation he once enjoyed while studying plants and insects in Charleston. In 1907, he graduated from Dartmouth with a dual major in biology and history. He was first in his class and the only student to graduate magna cum laude—with highest honors. Later that year, he accepted a teaching position at Howard University in Washington, D.C. and in 1912, was named head of the university's biology department.

While still at Howard, Ernest enrolled in a doctoral program at the University of Chicago where he was introduced to Dr. Frank R. Lillie, head of the department of zoology. Dr. Lillie invited Ernest to become his laboratory assistant at the Marine Biological Laboratory at Woods Hole, Massachusetts. During that time, biological research at Woods Hole was regarded highly, and many of the world's great biologists did work there. Ernest went to Woods Hole every summer for more than 20 years to do research. In the early 1930s, Ernest left Woods Hole to continue his work in Europe, where he felt he was better accepted. He returned to the United States in 1941 to teach at Howard University. He died later that year of cancer.

Ernest Just pioneered the study of cell life and human metabolism. He was one of the first to challenge popular scientific thinking about cell function and cell structure. He wrote many papers and several books. In 1915 the NAACP honored Ernest with the first Spingarn Award for his contributions.

MASSEY, WALTER EUGENE
PHYSICIST-ADMINISTRATOR

1938—
Birthplace: Hattiesburg, MS

Walter was the first African American to serve as president of the American Association for the Advancement of Science, the largest general science organization in the country. Then, in 1990, President George Bush selected him to head the National Science Foundation.

One would not expect that Walter would make such important contributions when he arrived at Morehouse College in 1954. The 16 year old became homesick and wanted to return home. But his mother insisted that he stay. Walter also received support and encouragement from the faculty at Morehouse. In high school he had not taken a single course in chemistry, advanced algebra, or trigonometry. But he applied himself and graduated with a bachelor's degree in physics and mathematics. He then earned a doctorate degree from Washington University in St. Louis, Missouri. While completing his doctoral work, Walter began working as a member of the research staff at Argonne National Laboratory, operated for the United States Department of Energy first by a group of universities, and then by the University of Chicago.

After receiving his doctorate degree, Walter held faculty positions at several prominent universities, including Brown University in Providence, Rhode Island, where he did his most significant academic research. In 1979, Walter was named director of the Argonne National Laboratory with a position as full professor at the University of Chicago. He assumed control of an annual budget of more than $250 million and a staff of almost 4,000. Many people thought that the laboratories that were responsible for much of our country's scientific research had no clear mission. Walter introduced participatory democracy, and established a related corporation that helped to transfer technologies created in the laboratory to industry and the marketplace.

From 1978 to 1984 Walter was member of the National Science Board. In 1995 Morehouse College, the nation's only historically Black, four-year college for men, selected Walter to serve as its president. It seemed fitting that this outstanding educator, scientist and administrator would be chosen to lead this important institution toward the next millennium.

McNair, Ronald
Physicist-Astronaut

1950—1986
Birthplace: Lake City, SC

The excitement could be felt everywhere. Only a few more minutes and the shuttle called *Challenger* would take off for its six-day flight through outer space. Among the seven astronauts selected for this important voyage of exploration was mission specialist Ronald McNair. This would be his second trip into space. In February, 1984, he also served as a mission specialist on an eight-day flight aboard *Mission 41-B*. Ronald was the second Black astronaut in space. Guion Bluford was the first.

But Ronald was excited about this space flight, too. He was going to operate the Spartan scientific package during observations of Haley's Comet.

Finally, the countdown began. Then a loud cheer rang out from the people who had gathered to see the launch as the *Challenger* blasted toward space. Soon, the cheers turned to tears and screams. Moments after take off, *Challenger* exploded, killing all seven astronauts aboard, including Ronald McNair.

Ronald grew up in a small town in South Carolina when legal segregation was nearing its end. His mother was a teacher and his father was an auto body repairman. Ronald graduated from Carver High School in 1967, and enrolled at North Carolina A & T University. He graduated with a degree in physics and went on to earn a doctorate degree in physics from the Massachusetts Institute of Technology (M.I.T.). He did research in laser physics while at M.I.T., and later in France. He joined the Hughes Research Laboratory in Malibu, California in 1976, and was working there as a scientist when he was one of 35 astronauts selected by NASA in January, 1978. In August, 1979, he completed training and an evaluation course that qualified him to be a shuttle mission specialist.

Some critics felt that the *Challenger* disaster would end America's commitment to explore and learn more about space. It did not. While the disaster did bring about changes in the space program, America was as committed as ever to explore space. Ronald McNair and the six other astronauts who lost their lives on that January day in 1986 would surely be proud.

TURNER, CHARLES HENRY
ENTOMOLOGIST

1867—1923
Birthplace: Cincinnati, OH

A s a youngster, Charles spent much of his free time analyzing the habits and behavior of insects. He could often be found crouched over anthills or stationed beneath a spiderweb watching the movements of the creatures.

After finishing high school, Charles attended the University of Cincinnati where he earned his bachelor's degree in 1891 and his master's degree a year later. In 1893 Charles moved to Atlanta, where he taught at Clark College for two years. After earning his doctorate from the University of Chicago in 1907, Charles turned his attention to teaching young people. He felt he was needed as a teacher and that through teaching, he could do more for his people. He became the biology teacher at Sumner High School in St. Louis, Missouri in 1908 and remained there until his death in 1923.

Charles was a devoted teacher, but during his off hours he conducted research and studied the behavior of insects. His research provided new understanding on how insects perceived the world. Charles proved that odor alone did not guide insects. He showed that bees relied on memory and that they could distinguish certain colors and patterns. Charles was also the first person to prove that insects could hear and distinguish pitch and that roaches learn by trial and error. He published more than 50 articles on insects' and animals' behavior.

Charles's most notable discovery was considered so remarkable within the scientific community that it was named in his honor. The term "Turner's Circling" refers to the unique turning movement some ants make as they try to find the way back to their nest. After his death in 1923 the St. Louis Board of Education built a school and named it in Charles Turner's honor.

TYSON, NEIL DEGRASSE
ASTROPHYSICIST

1948—
Birthplace: Bronx, NY

A strophysics is the branch of astronomy which deals primarily with the physical properties of universe. Today, there are more than 4,000 astrophysicists in the United States. Only a tiny fraction are African Americans. Neil de Grasse Tyson is one of that small number. Encouraged and supported by parents and friends, Neil achieved a childhood dream to become an astrophysicist.

Neil's interest in the subject began at an early age. Neil graduated from the Bronx High School of Science, where he was an outstanding athlete. But he didn't want to be a professional ball player. Having developed a keen interest in science as a youngster, Neil began to pursue his goal. He received a bachelor's degree in physics from Harvard University, a master's degree in astronomy from the University of Texas, and a doctorate degree in astrophysics from Columbia University. Along the way, Neil faced many obstacles. College faculty members and fellow students suggested that Neil pursue a career as a computer salesman or as a community college teacher. They didn't believe an African American could become an astrophysicist. But Neil didn't let this prejudice deter him. After graduating from Columbia, he was appointed to a research position at Princeton University's department of astrophysical sciences.

After spending a number of years doing important research in his field, Neil was appointed director of the American Museum of Natural History's Hayden Planetarium. He became the youngest director ever of one of the world's largest and most important planetariums. As head of Hayden, Neil directs the scientific research efforts of the planetarium and guides its educational outreach program. He also continues to do research, which he loves.

Neil de Grasse Tyson's childhood dream has come true. Today, he is one of the most respected and influential astrophysicists in the world. He has written a number of articles and books, including his autobiography, *The Sky Is Not the Limit*, published in 2000. Neil has also made many television and radio appearances where he has shared his vast knowledge of space.

HEALERS

PROVIDING TREATMENT, FINDING CURES

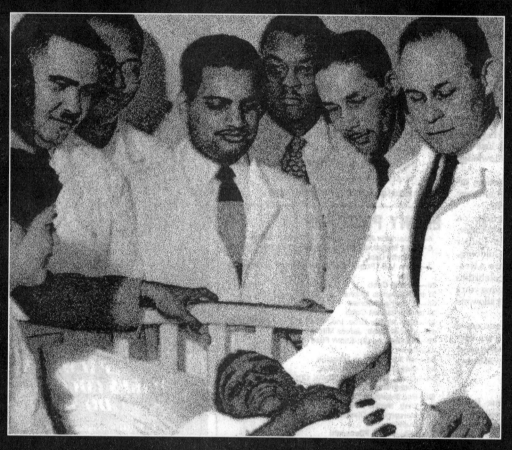

Dr. Charles Drew, surgeon and chief of staff at Freedman's Hospital, Washington, D.C., received the 1944 Spingarn Medal for his work on blood plasma.

"We'll start a hospital of our own and we'll train dozens and dozens of nurses. There must be a hospital for Negroes but not a Negro hospital."
— Dr. Daniel Hale Williams

BATH, PATRICIA
OPHTHALMOLOGIST

1942—
Birthplace: New York, NY

D r. Patricia Bath once said, "the ability to restore vision is the ultimate regard. It is a really great joy to remove eye patches the day after surgery and the patient can see again."

This desire to make a difference in the lives of others is what led Patricia to pursue a career as an ophthalmology surgeon. It also motivated her to invent a very important tool for eye surgery. In 1988, Patricia received patents for a laser cataract surgery device. This instrument is used in human cataract surgery. A cataract is a cloudiness of the lens of the eye that affects millions of people around the world. Before Patricia's invention, a mechanical drill-like tool was commonly used to grind away the cataract. Her laser cataract surgery device is much more accurate and effective.

Patricia was born in Harlem, New York, where her parents encouraged her love of learning. She was an excellent student in high school. As a National Science Foundation summer student, she participated in innovative work in cancer research that gained her national exposure. She graduated from Hunter College in New York in 1964 and Howard University Medical School in 1968. After completing her medical internship at Harlem Hospital in New York, she was awarded a fellowship in ophthalmology at Columbia University. Patricia was instrumental in bringing ophthalmic surgical services to Harlem Hospital's eye clinic. She also persuaded her professors to operate on blind patients at the clinic for free. In 1974 Patricia joined the faculty of the UCLA Medical School and the King-Drew Medical Center as assistant professor of surgery and ophthalmology. By 1983, Patricia was chair of the Ophthalmology Residency Training Program at UCLA/King-Drew, the first woman to ever hold such a position in the country.

Patricia retired from the UCLA Medical Center in 1993. Since then, she has devoted much of her time to finding ways to use electronic communication to provide medical service to remote areas where health care is limited. She is also president of the American Association for the Prevention of Blindness, an organization she helped to found, and is professor of ophthalmology at St. Georges University in Grenada.

CARSON, BENJAMIN
NEUROSURGEON

1951—
Birthplace: Detroit, MI

"After studying the available information, I tentatively agreed to do the surgery, knowing it would be the riskiest and most demanding thing I have ever done."— Dr. Benjamin Carson

T he year was 1987. Dr. Benjamin Carson was referring to a delicate operation to separate twins who were born joined at the back of their heads. Only 36 years old at the time, Dr. Carson had made a trip to West Germany to attempt this difficult procedure. Usually the separation of Siamese twins results in the death of one of them.

It took 22 hours of painstaking surgery, and several weeks of waiting, to see if the operation was successful. It was. Dr. Carson and a team of 70 doctors had accomplished what some have called "a medical miracle." But this was just one of the many complex and delicate operations Dr. Carson has performed as a neurosurgeon.

Ben Carson was born in Detroit, Michigan. His father left when he was eight years old, leaving his mother to raise him and his brother Curtis alone. At first, Ben and his brother were headed down the wrong path, but a reading program and the limited amount of television viewing their mother imposed on them put the boys on the right path. Ben became an avid reader and his grades improved greatly.

Ben always wanted to become a doctor. He excelled in high school and received a scholarship from Yale University. He graduated in 1973 and entered the University of Michigan School of Medicine. At first, Ben planned to become a psychotherapist, but during his first year of medical school he discovered neurosurgery. Ben did his internship in general surgery from 1977 to 1978 and his residency in neurosurgery from 1978 to 1982 at John Hopkins Hospital, one of the country's leading medical centers.

From 1982 to 1983, Ben was chief resident at John Hopkins. After spending two years at the Sir Charles Gairdner Hospital in Australia, Ben returned to John Hopkins. A year later he was named director of pediatric neurosurgery. At the age of 33, Ben was one of the youngest directors to head a surgical division in the United States.

Dr. Ben Carson has continued to take on difficult cases, performing operations that have saved countless lives. In a Readers Digest article, writer Christopher Phillips called this great surgeon "one of the acknowledged miracle workers of modern medicine."

CHINN, MAY EDWARD
PHYSICIAN

1896—1980
Birthplace: Great Barrington, MA

When May Chinn was a youngster growing up on the estate of the Tiffanys, a rich White family who lived in Tarrytown, New York, it seemed that she would pursue a career in music. Though May's mother worked for the Tiffanys, May was often treated as if she were a member of the family. She studied the classics with the Tiffany children and went to concerts with them. It was while she was living on the Tiffany estate that May's musical gifts were first nurtured.

May's mother had to find a new job after the Tiffanys sold their Tarrytown estate. May and her mother moved to New York City where May took piano lessons and attended school. After a while, May lost interest in school and dropped out. She found work as a piano teacher, giving lessons to elementary students. Later, May regained her interest in education, and with encouragement from her mother, she took and passed a high school equivalency exam. In 1917, she entered Columbia University's Teachers College where she majored in music. After her first year, Mae changed her major to science. While attending Columbia, May continued to play and sing in concerts around New York. She also played for Paul Robeson, the famous African-American concert performer.

In 1921, May graduated from Columbia. She decided she wanted to pursue a career in medicine. She enrolled at Bellevue Hospital Medical College, and in 1926 became the first African-American woman to obtain a medical degree from that school. May continued to achieve firsts. She was the African-American woman to become an intern at Harlem Hospital, and the first woman physician to ride with an ambulance crew on emergency calls. With other physicians in Harlem, she worked on staff at the Edgecombe Sanitarium.

During the later years of her career May worked at the Strang Clinic in New York City concentrating her efforts on the early detection and diagnosis of cancer. May Chinn retired from the Strang Clinic at age 81. But this hard working and determined woman didn't allow retirement to stop her. She continued to work in daycare centers in Harlem. May Edward Chinn died in 1980, after practicing medicine for over 50 years. She is still remembered as one of the pioneering African-American physicians.

COLE, REBECCA J.
PHYSICIAN

1846—1922
Birthplace: Unknown

Students of the Medical College for Women in the dissection room, 1870.

In the mid 18th century, women—Black and White—who were forced to live under the domination of males started to assert themselves. Many wanted to receive training in professions that were traditionally practiced by men. Medicine was one of these professions. In 1849, Elizabeth Blackwell became the first White woman to receive her medical degree. Fifteen years later, Rebecca Lee, an African-American woman, graduated from New England Medical College. She was closely followed by Rebecca Cole, also an African–American woman, who graduated from Women's Medical College of Pennsylvania in 1867. This early institution later became part of MCP-Hannheman University.

There is much speculation as to which doctor, Rebecca Lee or Rebecca Cole, was the first African-American woman physician to actually practice in the United States. Both were equally accomplished, but Rebecca Cole achieved some prominence for her work with Elizabeth Blackwell.

After graduating from medical school, Rebecca joined Elizabeth Blackwell at the New York Infirmary for Women and Children. In addition to running the infirmary, in 1866 Elizabeth and her sister Emily started the Blackwell Tenement House Service, the first medical social service program established in the United States. Rebecca Cole was one of the service's first "sanitary visitors." She made house calls to people living in slum neighborhoods and taught women the basics of good hygiene and childcare.

When Rebecca moved to Philadelphia, she continued her career in social medicine. She helped start the Woman's Directory, which provided medical and legal assistance to women. She practiced medicine in Philadelphia until 1881. Later she became the superintendent of the Home for Destitute Colored Women and Children in Washington, D.C.

Rebecca was outspoken about the state of Black health care. When W.E.B. DuBois publicly stated that he felt Blacks died of consumption in such high numbers because of their ignorance of hygiene, Rebecca disagreed, blaming slum landlords instead for the high mortality rates in poor areas. Rebecca Cole practiced medicine for 50 years and in that time built a lasting legacy of help and healing.

DREW, CHARLES
DIRECTOR OF BLOOD BANK

1904—1950
Birthplace: Washington, D.C.

Charles Richard Drew was an outstanding athlete. He excelled in track and football in high school and college and even served as a college football coach for several years. But medicine was always his main interest, and it was in medicine that he made his greatest contributions to the world.

As a young doctor Charles saw many patients go into shock and die because of blood loss. Transfusions of fresh blood might have saved their lives, but hospitals could not easily preserve fresh, ready-to-use blood. Stored blood would spoil quickly, thickening and forming clots that made it impossible to use. Charles's research led to a method that allowed blood and plasma, the fluid part of blood, to be stored for future use. The energetic and tireless young physician was also instrumental in setting up blood bank programs in England and for the American Red Cross. He was the first director of the blood bank program operated by the American Red Cross. Charles's accomplishments, however, didn't end there. He was the first African American to receive a doctor of science degree, which he earned from Columbia University.

Charles was born in Washington, D.C. His father was a carpet layer and his mother taught school until she retired to raise Charles and his four brothers and sisters. Following high school, Charles attended Amherst College in Massachusetts where he continued to excel in athletics. After graduating from Amherst, he did not have enough money for medical school, so he took a position at Morgan State College as director of athletics and a biology instructor. He continued to plan for medical school. Eventually, he was accepted to McGill University Medical School in Canada. After graduating, he interned for one year at Montreal General Hospital in Canada. It was there that his interest in the study of blood and the problems of blood transfusion grew. After completing his internship, Charles went to Howard University Medical School, where he was an instructor in pathology. While at Howard, he received a fellowship from the Rockefeller Foundation to do research in blood and blood transfusion. The rest is history. Charles's pioneering successes in blood research have saved countless lives worldwide.

ELDERS, JOCELYN
SURGEON GENERAL

1933—
Birthplace: Schaal, AK

At age 15, Minnie Jocelyn Jones entered Philander Smith College, a predominately Black institution located in Little Rock, Arkansas. That year, Jocelyn saw a doctor for the first time in her life. Her parents were sharecroppers and most sharecroppers didn't earn enough money to afford doctors. Jocelyn decided she was going to become physician.

In 1952 Jocelyn graduated from college after only three years. From there she went on to the University of Arkansas Medical School in Little Rock, Arkansas. She graduated in 1960, the only woman that year to do so. That year, she also married Oliver Elders. In 1961 she completed her internship at the University of Minnesota Hospital in Minneapolis and returned to Arkansas to do her residency. At the University of Arkansas Medical Center she rose to the position of chief pediatric resident, and was named a pediatric research fellow in 1964. In 1967, Jocelyn earned a master's degree in biochemistry and joined the faculty at the University of Arkansas Medical Center. In 1976, she became a full professor.

In 1987, then Arkansas Governor Bill Clinton appointed Jocelyn director of the state's department of health. She was responsible for overseeing public health programs and policies for the people of Arkansas. As director, she championed comprehensive health education and school-based clinics as effective programs for coping with teenage pregnancy. She also developed a comprehensive HIV testing and counseling program, increased breast cancer screenings, and campaigned for around-the-clock care for elderly and terminally ill patients.

In 1993, Bill Clinton, who was now President of the United States, nominated Jocelyn to serve as United States Surgeon General. After a lengthy process, Jocelyn was confirmed, becoming the first Black woman to serve in this important cabinet position.

Throughout Jocelyn's term as surgeon general, she was under attack from conservatives who did not like her outspokenness or her views on reproductive rights and sex education. She was asked to resign in December 1994. Jocelyn returned to the University of Arkansas for Medical Sciences, where she is a full professor on the faculty of the College of Medicine, Department of Pediatrics.

JOHNSON, HALLE TANNER
COLLEGE PHYSICIAN

1864—1901
Birthplace: Pittsburgh, PA

Halle Johnson was only 37 years old when she died from complications of childbirth and dysentery. But in her short life she did a lot to pave the way for women and African Americans in the field of medicine. Halle was not only the first African-American woman to be licensed to practice medicine in the state of Alabama, she was the first woman. She was also the first resident physician at Tuskegee Institute.

Halle was born in Pittsburgh, Pennsylvania, the oldest of nine children. One of her brothers was the famous painter Henry Ossawa Tanner.

Halle's mother and father created a wholesome learning environment for their children. They introduced them to art and culture. Halle's father, Benjamin, was an African Methodist Episcopal minister who later became a bishop in the church. He was also the first editor of the *A.M.E. Christian Review*, and Halle was a member of his staff.

In 1886, Halle married Charles E. Dillon. The following year, she gave birth to Sadie, the couple's only child. Then, Charles died. Halle was saddened, but she was determined to move on with her life. She enrolled in the Women's Medical College of Pennsylvania, the only African American in a class of 36 students. In 1891, after completing a three-year program, Halle graduated with high honors.

Booker T. Washington, president and founder of Tuskegee Institute in Alabama, had been searching for an African-American resident physician for a number of years. He offered Halle the job. She accepted. But first, Halle had to get her license. After taking a tough battery of tests, Halle received her medical license in one of the most segregated states in America.

Right away, she began her work at Tuskegee. From 1891 to 1894, she was a resident physician there. She established a nurses' training school and opened a dispensary which functioned like today's pharmacies. She also prepared a lot of the medicine. She remained at Tuskegee until she moved with her new husband, John Quincy Johnson, a mathematics instructor, to Princeton, New Jersey. John had been accepted to Princeton Theological Seminary to do postgraduate work. Afterward, the couple moved to Nashville, Tennessee, where John became a minister. Halle died in her Nashville home on April 26, 1901 giving birth to her second child. She will always be remembered as the first woman to be licensed to practice medicine in the state of Alabama.

KOUNTZ, SAMUEL K.
PIONEER TRANSPLANT SURGEON

1930—1981
Birthplace: Lexa, AK

Samuel L. Kountz was one of the world's most distinguished surgeons and a pioneer in the field of kidney transplantation. In 1961, while working with Dr. Roy Cohn at the Stanford University Medical Center, Samuel made history by transplanting a kidney from a mother to a daughter—the first successful transplant between humans who were not identical twins. The renowned surgeon performed more than 500 kidney transplants during his career, believed to be the most by any physician. He was also the first to discover that large doses of the drug methylprednisolone could help reverse the acute rejection of a transplanted kidney.

In 1967, Samuel was named associate professor of surgery and chief of the Kidney Transplant Service at the University of California, San Francisco. Later that year, he and other researchers developed the Belzer Kidney Perfusion Machine which could preserve a kidney from a donor for up to 50 hours. In 1972, he left California to accept the position of professor and chairperson of the department of surgery at the State University of New York's Downstate Medical Center in Brooklyn. Under Samuel's leadership, the organ transplant program at the Downstate Medical Center became one of the best in the nation.

Samuel first became interested in medicine when he went with a friend to a local hospital for emergency service. He was so moved by the doctor's ability to relieve suffering that he decided he would become a doctor. He was just eight years old. The Baptist boarding school Samuel attended did not prepare him for college, so he had to take remedial courses before entering the Arkansas Agricultural, Mechanical, and Normal College (AM&N).

In 1952, Samuel graduated third in his class at Arkansas AM&N. He applied to the all-White University of Arkansas Medical School, but was rejected. So he pursued his master's degree in chemistry at the University of Arkansas, Fayette campus. Two years later, in 1954, he was awarded a full scholarship to the University of Arkansas Medical School and became its first African-American student. In 1959, he began his surgical training at Stanford University School of Medicine. At Stanford, Samuel studied under Dr. Roy Cohn, one of the pioneers in the field of organ transplantation. It was there that Samuel decided to make transplant surgery his life's work.

LAWLESS, THEODORE K.
DERMATOLOGIST

1892—1971
Birthplace: Thibodeaux, LA

T heodore Kenneth Lawless, who achieved international acclaim as a dermatologist, set up his office in the heart of the Black community in Chicago's South Side. But people from all racial and economical backgrounds came to him in search of cures and treatments for skin disorders. Dr. Lawless was successful in treating many of them. During his long career, he gained recognition around the world for his research into the treatment of syphilis, leprosy, sporotrichosis, and many other skin diseases. He was also one of the first doctors to use radium in the treatment of cancer.

Theodore was the oldest son of a minister. As a youngster growing up in Louisiana during the turn of the century, he worked as an assistant to a veterinarian. It was during that time he decided he wanted to be involved in medicine.

After graduating from Talladega College in Alabama, Theodore spent two years at the medical school of the University of Kansas. Then he transferred to Northwestern University, where he earned his medical degree in 1919. After completing a year of additional study in dermatology and syphilology, Theodore began to do extensive work at a number of prestigious universities and hospitals in the United States and in Europe. He established his own practice in Chicago in 1924, and continued to do medical research at Northwestern University.

Like most African Americans during that period, Theodore faced racial prejudice and discrimination. He did not receive the proper respect and recognition due a doctor of his stature from his colleagues at Northwestern. He was prevented from opening an office on Chicago's famous "Loop," so he established his practice on the South Side, where it remained for more than forty years.

Theodore donated generously to educational institutions, and provided scholarships for Black students. In 1954, the NAACP presented him with the 39th Spingarn Medal for his "notable contributions to the health, enlightenment, and welfare of his fellow citizens of all races, faiths, and classes."

MAHONEY, MARY ELIZA
NURSE

1845—1926
Birthplace: Boston, MA

Before the latter part of the 19th century, many American nurses were untrained. Doctors were often not available, so these women delivered babies and provided folk remedies for illnesses. In the North and South, many of these nurses were Black. African-American women had long been nurses and midwives in the United States. Yet when nursing schools started opening after the Civil War, Black women were usually not allowed to attend them.

Mary Eliza Mahoney was an exception. She was the first African-American woman to graduate from a professional White nursing school. Mary's interest in nursing began when, as the oldest daughter in a family of 25, she acted as midwife at the births of her younger brothers and sisters. But it wasn't until she was 33 years old that she was accepted at the New England Hospital for Women and Children in Boston, the first American school to introduce a nursing program. Dr. Marie Zakrzewska was the head of the school, and she was a firm believer in equal rights for women and for Blacks. Under her guidance, six Black nurses graduated by 1899. Mary Mahoney was the first.

The nursing course lasted 16 months, and Mary, a small, energetic young woman, worked 16 hours a day, seven days a week. The only Black woman in her class, Mary washed, ironed, cleaned, scrubbed, and studied, which was what all the student nurses were expected to do. The courses and the physical work were so difficult, only three students out of that class of 42 graduated.

Mary worked as a nurse for 40 years after her graduation in 1879. She also helped other graduate nurses as much as she could. In 1936, the National Association of Colored Graduate Nurses established the Mary Mahoney Award to recognize Mary's ceaseless efforts to assist the organization and nurses in general. The Mary Mahoney Award is given to those African-American nurses who have contributed much to their profession—like Mary did more than one hundred years ago.

REID, CLARICE D.
SICKLE CELL
ADMINISTRATOR

1931—
Birthplace: Birmingham, AL

S ickle-cell anemia is a disease of the blood that occurs primarily in people of African descent. It affects one out of five hundred Black babies born in the United States. Victims of the disease suffer great pain, infections, and strokes. They often die young and as yet there is no known cure.

Since the disease was discovered here in the United States in 1910, doctors from all over the world have been searching for a cure. Until one is found, all they can do is help sickle-cell sufferers live with the disease.

Dr. Clarice Reid is one of those doctors. She has always been interested in the health problems of minorities. In medical school, where she was the only Black student, she specialized in pediatrics and family medicine. This allowed her to learn about the diseases that affect children and their families. After graduating from the University of Cincinnati Medical School in 1959, Clarice became the only African-American pediatrician in private practice in Cincinnati, Ohio.

Meanwhile, a lot of exciting research was being done in the area of sickle-cell anemia at Howard University in Washington, D.C. Clarice went to Washington and her interest in helping sickle-cell patients grew. As the deputy director of the sickle-cell program of the Health Service Administration, and later with the National Heart, Lung and Blood Institute Clarice helped to make people, particularly African Americans, aware of the disease. She developed a national program to reduce the death rate from the disease, and has taught nurses, social workers, and other health professionals how to care for sickle-cell patients.

Because of Clarice Reid's work, the care for people with sickle cell anemia has greatly improved in the past 20 years. The life span and the quality of life for these patients have improved as well.

Dr. Clarice Reid has received many honors for her work, including the Public Health Service Superior Service Award, which is the highest honor given by the United States Public Health Service. She retired in 1998.

SATCHER, DAVID ANDREW
SURGEON GENERAL

1941—
Birthplace: Anniston, AL

For four years David Satcher served as surgeon general of the United States. He also served as assistant secretary for health. He was just the second person in history to hold that position and serve simultaneously as surgeon general. His term began in February, 1998 and ended February, 2002. As the nation's 16th surgeon general, David served as the leading spokesman on matters related to public health. He was the second African American to head the surgeon general's office. Jocelyn Elders served as surgeon general from 1994 to 1996.

David has had a long and distinguished career in public health and public health education. A 1963 graduate of Morehouse College in Atlanta, Georgia, he received his master's and doctorate degrees from Case Western Reserve University. He did his residency and fellowship training at Strong Memorial Hospital, University of Rochester, UCLA Medical School and the Dr. Martin Luther King, Jr./Charles R. Drew Medical School.

From 1977 to 1979, David served as the interim dean of the Charles R. Drew Postgraduate Medical School and directed the King-Drew Sickle Cell Research Center. From 1970 to 1982, he was a professor in and chairman of the Department of Community Medicine and Family Practice at Morehouse College. He was chosen to serve as president of Meharry Medical College, in Nashville, Tennessee, a position he held from 1982 to 1993.

Prior to David Satcher's selection as surgeon general, he directed the Center for Disease Control and Prevention and was administrator of the Agency for Toxic Substances and Disease Registry. He served in those capacities from 1993 to 1998.

When the country's new president, George W. Bush, took office, David's term as surgeon general ended and he was appointed a fellow at the Kaiser Family Foundation. In the fall of 2002, David was selected to head the National Center for Primary Care at the Morehouse School of Medicine in Atlanta, Georgia.

STEWART, SUSAN McKINLEY
PHYSICIAN

1848—1918
Birthplace: Brooklyn, NY

S usan Maria Smith was the third African-American woman to receive a medical degree in the United States, and the first in the state of New York. For years, this dedicated physician brought quality health care to Black and White, rich and poor in Brooklyn and Manhattan, New York. She also helped found a hospital for women and children.

The seventh of ten children, as a child, Susan was interested in music. But as she grew older, she became interested in medicine. The chance of an African-American woman becoming a doctor in the post-Civil War era was nearly impossible. There were only two Black female doctors in the entire country at the time. But a determined Susan decided she was going to give it a try. In 1867, the 20-year-old entered New York Medical College and Hospital for Women in New York City. She was the first Black woman to attend the medical college. She graduated in 1870, after three years of study.

A short while later Susan opened an office in Brooklyn, where she had grown up. The office was located not too far from Bridge Street A.M.E. Church where she would later serve as choir director.

At first, few people came to her office. Some did not trust a female doctor. But as her patients spread the word about the excellent care Susan provided, her practice grew. Susan maintained her office in Brooklyn for 24 years. Later, she opened an office in Manhattan. In 1881, the tireless physician helped to found the Brooklyn Women's Homeopathic Hospital and Dispensary. The hospital was later renamed the Memorial Hospital for Women and Children.

In 1871, Susan married William G. McKinley. The couple had two children. William died in 1890, and three years later, Susan married Reverend Theophilus Gould Stewart, a chaplain of the 25th US Colored Infantry. Susan traveled with her husband to different forts where she treated many Black soldiers.

During a period when many doubted the ability of women in many different professions, Susan McKinley Stewart proved that women can be, and are, just as competent as men. In 1974, a junior high school in Brooklyn was named in her honor. A group of African-American doctors also paid tribute to this trailblazing physician by organizing the Susan Mckinley Stewart Medical Society.

TAYLOR, SUSIE KING
CIVIL WAR NURSE

1848—1912
Birthplace: Isle of Wight, GA

S usie King Taylor was raised by her grandmother in Savannah, Georgia. Even though she was born into slavery and was not allowed an education, she was taught how to read and write by a free Black woman. Understanding how important education was, 14-year-old Susie used her skills to teach other African Americans at the Freedman's School.

In 1862, President Abraham Lincoln signed the Emancipation Proclamation, which legally abolished slavery in the Confederate states. Even though Black soldiers were not allowed to fight alongside White soldiers and were treated badly, they fought bravely for their freedom and for their country.

Susie's husband, Edward King, was one of those soldiers. After they married in 1862, the couple moved to Port Royal Island off the South Carolina coast where Edward joined the First South Carolina Volunteers, an all-Black U.S. Army regiment. This regiment was made up of former slaves from the Sea Islands and was one of the first Black military units raised by the Lincoln administration.

Like all Black regiments, the First South Carolina Volunteers desperately needed medical assistance. Susie was working as a laundress for her husband's company. Although she had no formal training, she quickly offered her services and became the first Black army nurse to serve her country. Later, other Black women, including Harriet Tubman and Sojourner Truth, joined the troops to nurse their men. But Susie is believed to be the first. In addition to nursing the soldiers, Susie also took the time to teach the men how to read and write.

Edward King died at the end of the Civil War and Susie moved to Boston. There she met and married Russell Taylor in 1879. Susie was a volunteer nurse on the battlefront for four years, tending to the wounded soldiers, but received no pay and no pension for her dedicated work. In 1902, Susie published her memoirs, *My Life in Camp with the 33rd United States Colored Troops*.

WATTLETON, FAYE
WOMEN'S REPRODUCTIVE HEALTH ADVOCATE

1943—
Birthplace: St. Louis, MO

A lice Faye Wattleton's father was a factory worker, and her mother was a seamstress who also preached at a local church. Faye's mother felt that her daughter should be a missionary nurse, and go abroad to Africa and other parts of the world to serve the suffering. Although she didn't follow her mother's plan, Faye Wattleton was a missionary nonetheless. As a crusader for the reproductive rights of women, she has impacted the lives of thousands. For 14 years, from 1978 to 1992, she served as president of the Planned Parenthood Federation of America (PPFA), one of the country's most visible public health groups. She was the first African American and the first woman to head this important organization.

Faye was born in St. Louis, Missouri. After graduating from high school at age 16, she entered Ohio State University Nursing School where she received her degree in 1964. She then worked for two years as a maternity nursing instructor at the Miami Valley Hospital School of Nursing. While there, she learned about illegal abortions and the consequences of unwanted pregnancies. In 1966, she entered Columbia University in New York City and earned a master's degree in maternal and infant health care.

When Faye moved to Dayton, Ohio, she began to volunteer her time at the Planned Parenthood of Miami Valley. Her position as consultant and assistant director of Public Health Nursing Services in the Public Health Department of Dayton brought her face to face with the problem of illegal abortions and teenage pregnancy. She wanted to do something about the problem. Several years later, Faye was asked to take over as executive director of the Planned Parenthood of Miami Valley. Under her direction, the organization's budget rose to almost $1 million, and the number of women the organization served tripled. Faye's success led to her election as chair of the national executive directors' council of the Planned Parenthood Federation of America in 1975. Three years later she was chosen as president of the Planned Parenthood Federation of America.

Under her leadership, PPFA played a major role in shaping family planning policies and advocating on behalf of women and children. Faye resigned from her post in 1992, and recently established the Center for Gender Equality, a think tank focussing on women's issues. Her memoir, *Life on the Line*, was published in 1996. Missionary? Yes! But not in a foreign land, right here in her own country.

WILLIAMS, DANIEL HALE
OPEN HEART SURGEON

1856—1931
Birthplace: Holidayburg, PA

On July 9, 1893, James Cornish was rushed to Chicago's Provident Hospital with a stab wound to the heart. Dr. Daniel Hale Williams began to operate in an attempt to save the man's life. Other doctors had performed heart operations before, but no patient had survived such a delicate procedure. Amazingly, Cornish survived. Daniel Hale Williams had made history.

Medicine was not Daniel's first career choice. His father died and left his mother with seven children. Unable to care for them by herself, Daniel's mother sent her children to live with relatives. While living with his sister, Daniel was befriended by an African American who owned a barbershop. Daniel thought he wanted to be a barber, too. Later he thought he wanted to be a law clerk. At age 22 he became an apprentice to a Dr. Henry Palmer, a highly successful doctor. That's when he discovered the career he truly wanted to pursue. Daniel stayed with Dr. Palmer for two years, learning to be a doctor and scrubbing up the office at the end of the day. He could have opened his own office after his two-year apprenticeship, but Daniel was determined to be the best doctor he could be. With a loan he secured from a bank, he enrolled in Chicago Medical College, one of the best medical schools in the country at that time. He graduated in 1883 and opened an office in Chicago. In his practice, Daniel focused more and more on surgery. Because Black doctors and nurses were barred from working in White hospitals, Daniel performed most of his operations in private homes. His results were excellent, and his reputation as a successful surgeon grew.

Concerned about the lack of quality medical care for African Americans and the lack of opportunities for African-American doctors and nurses, he spearheaded an effort that resulted in the establishment of the Provident Hospital and Training School for Nurses. Founded in 1891 the hospital provided care to patients of all colors. During his long career, Daniel also served as chief surgeon at Howard University's Freedman's Hospital in Washington, D.C., and he became the first African American to be appointed associate attending surgeon at St. Luke's Hospital in Chicago. He retired in 1920.

Daniel Hale Williams will be remembered as a great surgeon, founder of one of the first interracial hospitals, and as a champion for the training of African-American nurses and doctors in the United States.

WILLIS, HAYES EMIL
COMMUNITY HEALTH CARE PIONEER

1947—1998
Birthplace: Portsmouth, VA

H ayes Emil Willis was always concerned about all people receiving quality health care. Like Dr. Daniel Hale Williams and other African-American pioneers in medicine, he was not simply satisfied with establishing a lucrative career for himself. He was moved by the unnecessary suffering many people endured because they didn't have access to quality health care. Like Dr. Williams, who established a hospital in Chicago that served all people, Hayes did something about the problem. He helped to establish a medical care facility, the South Richmond Health Center, which integrated primary care and public health services into a community-based site, bringing quality health care to the underserved population of that area of Richmond.

Born in Portsmouth, Virginia, when segregation was still the law, Hayes's father, a district manager for a Black insurance company and his mother, a schoolteacher, were his early role models. Hayes was an excellent student who finished third in his class in high school and won yearly state-wide science fair competitions. He earned a scholarship to Mount Union College in Ohio and graduated with honors in 1968. In 1975, after doing further study in biochemistry at Seton Hall University, he received his M.D. from Virginia Commonwealth University/Medical College of Virginia (MCV). He did his internship and residency in internal medicine at MCV and later joined the faculty. Subsequently, he became an assistant professor of rheumatology with a specialization in immunology. Interns, particularly African Americans and other people of color, sought Hayes as a mentor and he was always accessible.

Early in his career, Hayes concentrated on biomedical research and made major contributions in that field. Later, he began to focus on finding effective ways to deliver quality health care to underserved populations.

A member of numerous state and local medical committees and organizations, including the Governor's Task Force on Science and Technology, Hayes still found other ways to make a difference. He served as medical director at the Richmond Nursing Home and helped to bring quality care to a segment of the population that could least afford it.

Hayes Willis died January 6, 1998 following a two-year struggle with lymphoma. A few months later, the center he helped to found was renamed in his honor. The Hayes E. Willis Medical Center is now being used as a prototype by other cities and health organizations concerned about delivering quality health care to all citizens.

WRIGHT, JANE C.
CANCER RESEARCHER

1919—
Birthplace: New York, NY

As a little girl, Jane Wright had big footsteps in which to follow. Her father, Louis Tompkins Wright, was one of the country's outstanding surgeons and medical researchers. He was also an important force in the civil rights movement and served as chairman of the National Board of Directors of the NAACP. Sometimes having a famous parent is difficult for a child. This was not the case with Jane. Her father's outstanding career was an inspiration to her. She was motivated to excel.

Three years after graduating from New York Medical College in 1945, Jane joined the Harlem Hospital Cancer Research Foundation, which her father had founded. There she worked as a clinician. After her father's death in 1952, Jane succeeded him as director of the foundation. She concentrated her efforts on research, studying the effects of chemotherapy on tumors and other abnormal growths.

In 1955, Jane was named director of cancer chemotherapy and adjunct associate professor of research surgery at New York University School of Medicine. Two years later in 1957, she was appointed associate dean and professor of surgery at New York Medical College, the highest position ever held by an African-American woman in a medical administration at that time.

Jane has published 124 scientific papers and has written chapters for nine textbooks on cancer and cancer research. In 1975, the American Association for Cancer Research honored Jane for her important contributions to research in clinical cancer chemotherapy.

Although Jane is retired, she still leads an active life. She is professor emeritus of surgery at New York Medical College. In 1983, Jane was featured in a Smithsonian Institute exhibit entitled, "Black Women: Achievements Against the Odds." Like her father, Jane has become a role model for other young African-American scientists and doctors.

WRIGHT, LOUIS TOMPKINS
PIONEER PHYSICIAN

1891—1952
Birthplace: La Grange, GA

D r. Louis T. Wright achieved many firsts during his long career as a surgeon and physician. A true pioneer in medicine, he was the first Black physician to be appointed to the staff of a New York municipal hospital, the first physician to experiment with the antibiotic aureomycin on humans, and the first Black physician to head a public interracial hospital.

Louis specialized in surgery associated with head injuries and fractures. He devised a neck brace for neck fractures that is still used today. In 1943 he became director of surgery at Harlem Hospital in New York City. When Louis died from a heart attack in 1952, he was director of the Harlem Hospital Cancer Research Foundation. His daughter Jane succeeded him.

Louis's father, a graduate of Meharry Medical College, died when Louis was 4 years old. His mother was left with the responsibility of taking care of the family. She did so by working as a matron in the girls' dormitory at Clark College in Atlanta. Louis received his elementary, secondary and college education at Clark. When Louis was 8 years old, his mother married Dr. William Fletcher Penn, the first Black man to graduate from Yale Medical School. Dr. Penn inspired and encouraged Louis to pursue a career in medicine.

Louis graduated from Clark in 1911 and applied to Harvard Medical School. He was told that if he passed an examination in chemistry, he would be accepted. Louis passed the exam easily. He graduated from the Harvard Medical School cum laude, and fourth in his class. Unable to get an internship in Boston because White hospitals didn't accept Blacks there, he went to Freedman's Hospital in Washington, D.C., a hospital for Blacks.

During World War I, Louis served as a first lieutenant in the medical corps for the U.S. Army and introduced a new vaccination method for smallpox. When the war ended he was awarded a Purple Heart. Following the war, he opened an office in New York City. Four White doctors resigned in protest when Louis was appointed to a low-level position at Harlem Hospital. During that time, Harlem was a wealthy, White community. Louis was the first Black to be appointed to any position at a New York City hospital. Louis was associated with Harlem Hospital for more than thirty years.

In 1940 Louis was awarded a Spingarn Medal by the NAACP for his contributions to medical science and his fight for equal rights for Blacks.

INVENTORS

USING INGENUITY AND CREATIVITY

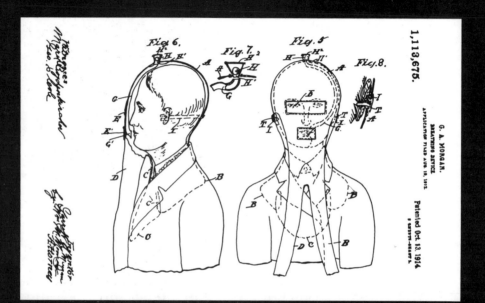

Drawing for Garrett A. Morgan's
Breathing Device

"The object of the invention is to provide a portable
attachment which will enable a fireman to enter a house
filled with thick, suffocating gases and smoke and to
breathe freely for some time therein, and thereby enable
him to perform his duties of saving life and valuables
without danger to himself from suffocation."
— Garrett A. Morgan

BEARD, ANDREW J.
INVENTOR

1849—1941
Birthplace:
Jefferson County, Alabama

Andrew Jackson Beard was an industrious man who possessed an adventuresome and entrepreneurial spirit. Andrew never went to school, but he was a quick learner. Born into slavery in 1849 in Jefferson County, Alabama, he was freed in 1865 at the end of the Civil War.

Like thousands of other newly freed African Americans, Andrew was finally able to pursue his own dreams. First, he operated a farm near Birmingham, Alabama. Five years later he used the money he earned selling bushels of apples to build a flourmill in Hardwicks, Alabama. Later, he started a real estate business that enjoyed modest success.

But it was as an inventor that Andrew made his mark. Andrew's first invention was a plow. He sold the patent in 1884 for $4,000. Another plow patent earned him $5,200 in 1887. Andrew's most important invention, however, was the automatic railroad coupler, also known as the Jenny Coupler.

Prior to Andrew's invention, coupling railroad cars was a dangerous job. A worker had to brace himself between two railway cars and drop a metal spike into a slot as the cars crashed together. Men were often injured when they could not move their arm or hand away from the colliding cars fast enough. Some even lost their lives when they fell between the two cars.

Andrew worked night and day to find a solution to the dangerous problem. In 1897, he found an answer. Andrew's automatic railroad coupler allowed trains to be joined together without human assistance. He got a patent and sold the rights to his new invention to a New York manufacturing firm for more than $50,000. Among Andrew's other inventions was a rotary steam engine that was patented in 1892.

CROSTHWAIT, DAVID NELSON, JR.

MECHANICAL ENGINEER

1898—1976
Birthplace: Kansas City, KS

As a youngster, the Black scientist and astronomer Benjamin Banneker spent long hours watching the stars at night. George Washington Carver could usually be found in the woods studying flowers, insects and plants. George Carruthers, the Black scientist who invented a special camera that has been used in space exploration, enjoyed spending time at the local planetarium. Like those important African Americans, David Nelson Crosthwait, Jr. developed an early interest in a field he would later choose as a career.

As a youngster growing up in Kansas City, Kansas, he knew that he wanted to be an engineer. While other youngsters played games, David designed and built intricate mechanical devices. Teachers who taught at the segregated, run-down school David attended during the early part of the century encouraged the energetic student to always do his best. When David graduated from high school, he received a full academic scholarship to Purdue University, a prestigious university with an excellent engineering program. David graduated at the top of his class, receiving a Bachelor of Science degree in engineering. Later, he received a Master of Science degree in mechanical engineering.

David began his career in 1925, working for the C. A. Dunham Company in Indiana. He was responsible for designing and installing heating systems and for diagnosing their problems when something went wrong.

David remained with the Dunham Company for 45 years. He patented more than 50 inventions while he worked there. One of them was a gigantic heating system for Radio City Music Hall in New York City.

David died in 1986 at the age of 88. In spite of a system that tried to ensure an inferior education for African Americans, David Crosthwait, Jr. made important contributions because of his hard work, determination, and because of the encouragement and support he received from his teachers and family.

HARVARD, CLAUDE
MECHANICAL ENGINEER

1911—1999
Birthplace: Dunlin, GA

A machine shop teacher noticed Claude Harvard's interest in machines and electronics. Claude and his family had moved from rural Georgia to Detroit, Michigan, the automobile capital of the world. Claude's teacher told Claude about the Ford Trade School started by Henry Ford to train orphaned children to be tool-and-die makers for his company. The principal of the school was so impressed with Claude that he admitted the bright student even though he was not an orphan. Claude graduated at the top of his class.

Graduates of the school were automatically issued a union card. Not Claude. Even with the assistance of the school principal, Claude was not able to secure a union card. Ford Motor Company had to create a job to utilize his talent. Claude, who had developed an early interest in radio, was eventually given a position as head of a radio department.

Claude went on to invent more than 26 devices that were patented by the Ford Motor Company. One of his inventions earned $250,000 for Ford when the company sold it to the United States Steel Company. All Ford employees had to surrender the rights to any inventions that were created while on the job.

One of Claude's most important inventions for Ford was an inspection machine. This device cleaned the surfaces of auto pistons and examined them with a magnetic pickup. It also inspected pistons for proper hardness and for defects. The machine marked a critical advancement in automobile safety.

Claude left Ford to form his own company, which was successful for a short while. Some of Claude Harvard's inventions revolutionized automobile manufacturing. Unfortunately, he never received the financial rewards he deserved. But people like Claude have made life easier and better for all of us.

JONES, FREDERICK McKINLEY
INDUSTRIAL ENGINEER

1892—1961
Birthplace: Cincinnati, OH

Frederick McKinley Jones had more than 20 patents for inventions he created during his lifetime. His two most notable inventions were the first automatic refrigeration system, and a ticket-dispensing machine for movie houses.

Although Frederick only got as far as the eighth grade, he was extremely bright and inventive. Orphaned at the age of 10, he lived in the home of a priest in Covington, Kentucky, until he was 16. Then he left to make his own way in life. He held a number of odd jobs, including working as a mechanic for an auto shop. He enjoyed working on engines and mastering the inner working of intricate machines. In 1917, near the end of World War I, Frederick joined the United States Army. There he learned about electrical wiring. Following his stint in the Army, Frederick moved to Minnesota, where he was offered a job by Joseph Numero, whose company manufactured motion picture equipment. In 1928, while still working for the company, he invented a ticket-dispensing machine. He received a patent for another version of the machine in 1939.

For many years, companies that transported perishable food to different parts of the country lost a lot of money. They lost money because the ice that was used to keep the food cool would often melt before reaching its destination. Frederick took up the challenge of finding a solution to the problem.

For several years Frederick worked to find an answer. He immersed himself in books about refrigeration. Finally, he completed a portable air conditioner for trucks and railway cars, and received a patent for it in July 1949. Several weeks later, he received a patent for a portable refrigeration system engine. Frederick's invention was sought by trucking companies, airlines, railroad companies, and grocery stores everywhere. Frederick and Joseph Numero formed a company to manufacture the new refrigeration system. They named it the United States Thermo Control Company. It became a multi-million dollar business. Frederick made a number of improvements on his original invention and received patents for them. Because of his invention, perishable food could be transported to all parts of the world.

LATIMER, LEWIS HOWARD
ELECTRICAL ENGINEER

1848—1928
Birthplace: Chelsea, MA

Lewis Howard Latimer loved to draw and had a talent for painting. When Crosby and Gould, patent lawyers, advertised for an office boy, Lewis applied for the job and got it. The law firm secured patents for inventors. Patents had to be accompanied by detailed drawings and draftsmen were used to make the drawings. Lewis gradually learned drafting techniques and convinced his employers to let him make drawings of some of the patents. His work was outstanding and he was given a job as a draftsman.

Alexander Graham Bell, creator of the telephone, was one inventor with whom Lewis worked. Bell needed a draftsman to assist him with the patent application and he asked Lewis to help him with it. Lewis did the drawings and assisted in preparing the descriptions needed to complete the application for Bell's invention. The patent was issued in 1876.

Soon, Lewis began working on inventions of his own. One of his earliest was a water closet or toilet for railroad cars, patented in 1874. In 1879, Thomas A. Edison invented the incandescent electric lamp, which ushered in a new age of electric lighting for the world. In 1881, Lewis and Joseph V. Nichols, his business partner, received a patent for their own electric lamp. Lewis and Nichols's invention dealt with a method of mounting the carbon filaments or connecting them to the metal wires in the lamp. But perhaps the most important of Lewis's many inventions was a process for manufacturing carbon filaments that resulted in a superior filament that lasted much longer than the ones Edison made from other materials. The patent to Lewis's invention was assigned to his employer, the United States Electric Lighting Company. Soon, Lewis was called upon to install some of the first incandescent electric light plants in New York City. Later he was sent to London to set up an incandescent lamp department for the Maxim-Weston Electric Company. Then, in 1884, Lewis received an offer from Thomas Edison to work with the engineering department of the Edison Electric Light Company. In 1890 he was transferred to the legal department, where he was of tremendous value to Edison, defending his patents as an expert witness.

The son of escaped slaves who made their way from Virginia to Massachusetts, Lewis Howard Latimer made many contributions to better the lives of people everywhere.

MATZELIGER, JAN ERNST
INDUSTRIAL ENGINEER

1853—1889
Birthplace: Paramaribo, Surinam

B efore Jan Ernst Matzeliger invented the shoelasting machine, most people could not afford shoes. They were too expensive. It took a long time to finish making each shoe. The most difficult part was connecting the upper part to the innersole. This step was called lasting and it had to be done by hand. The leather had to be stretched over a wooden model of a foot called a last, then the finished shape had to be tacked into place onto the sole. There was no machine to do this important work. Jan decided he was going to invent such a machine.

Born in South America, Jan's father was White and his mother was Black. While working in his father's shop, Jan learned how to use the lathe machine, which cut and shaped metal. When he turned 19, he sailed on a ship to the Far East. Two years later the ship docked in the city of Philadelphia. Despite the experience he had gained working in his father's shop, Jan found it difficult to secure work in Philadelphia. He finally landed a job with a shoemaker. There he learned to operate the McKay machine, which sewed leather together to make the soles of shoes.

In 1877, Jan moved to Lynn, Massachusetts, the city that was called the "shoe industry capital of the world." Jan was hired at the Harney Brothers' factory. It was while working for Harney Brothers that Jan got the idea to make a lasting machine.

By the fall of 1880, Jan had made a model of a lasting machine from cigar boxes. Another inventor offered him $50 for it. Jan said no. He knew he had created something very special. By 1882, Jan had made a model of his invention from scrap metal. It lasted shoes perfectly. This time, Jan was offered $1,500 for his invention. Again he said no. Two businessmen gave Jan the money he needed to make his machine from new metal parts. The three partners formed the Union Lasting Machine Company. On March 20, 1883, Jan was given a patent for his new invention. Jan's lasting machine could last from 300 to 700 shoes in a ten-hour work-day. One person doing the same work by hand could finish only 50 pairs of shoes in that time. Many people got rich because of Jan's invention, but he was soon forgotten. But he had made a contribution that changed the shoe industry and made shoes widely available.

McCoy, Elijah
Mechanical Engineer

1843—1929
Birthplace: Colchester, Ontario, Canada

Most inventions are created to address a need. That was the reason Elijah McCoy developed his most important invention, the "lubricator cup." Among the responsibilities Elijah had while working for a railroad company was oiling the moving parts of trains. Every few miles a train would stop so the parts could be oiled. If the parts were not oiled, they could rub together, stick, and then stop the train from moving. Elijah decided to find a better way to lubricate the moving parts.

In 1872, Elijah found the answer: a cup that would drip oil to the parts that needed lubricating. Later that year, Elijah received a patent for his invention.

At first, railroad executives did not accept Elijah's invention. They didn't believe a Black man was smart enough to create such an important tool. One company decided to try the new invention, and it worked well. Word spread about the lubricating cup. Soon, all railroad companies wanted Elijah's invention. Others tried to copy Elijah's device, but theirs did not work as well. Companies knew the difference and demanded the "real McCoy," a phrase that is still used today to indicate the "real thing."

Elijah's mother and father were escaped slaves who made their way to freedom in Canada. Elijah was born in Colchester, Ontario, Canada. When Elijah was 16 years old, he went to school in Scotland to learn drafting. He also studied engineering. He finished his training and became a master mechanic and engineer.

When Elijah moved to Ypsilanti, Michigan, he could not find a job. Even though slavery had ended, African Americans still faced discrimination and prejudice. So despite his training, Elijah had to accept a job as a fireman and oilman for the Michigan Central Railroad. It was while he was working for the railroad company that he invented the lubricator cup.

In 1882, Elijah began to work full time as an inventor. Among his other inventions were an ironing board and a lawn sprinkler. In all, Elijah received 57 patents for his inventions.

Elijah died in 1929 while living in a home for the poor and elderly. He had used all the money he had earned trying to improve his many inventions. The city of Detroit honored him in 1975, naming a street in his honor.

MORGAN, GARRETT A.
INVENTOR

1877—1963
Birthplace: Paris, Kentucky

G arrett Morgan barely completed elementary school, but his genius and ingenuity was second to none. He gave the world two very important inventions, the gas mask and the traffic signal, both of which have saved the lives of thousands of people.

Garrett Augustus Morgan was born in Kentucky, the seventh of eleven children. He left home when he was 14 years old and moved to Cincinnati, Ohio. Unable to find work in Cincinnati, he moved to Cleveland, Ohio. There he worked as a sewing machine adjuster, and saved enough money to open his own tailoring business. It was a successful operation that at one time employed 32 workers.

Garrett's first invention, a chemical to straighten hair, happened by chance. He discovered the solution while he was experimenting with a lubricant to reduce the fiction that needles created when they were used with sewing machines. The formula didn't prevent the fiction, but to Garrett's amazement, it straightened hair. Garrett patented the formula and in 1913, formed the G. A. Morgan Refining Company to manufacture and market his new product.

In 1914, Garrett received a patent for his gas mask, which he called the "gas inhalator." It was later called a safety hood. In 1916, Garrett and his brother Frank used the invention to save the lives of workers trapped by smoke and fire in a tunnel. After that, people everywhere wanted to see the funny-looking masks that would allow someone to walk safely into a smoke-filled area. Fire departments and mining companies were very interested, too. during World War I, American soldiers used the masks to protect themselves from poisonous gas after the government made some changes to the original invention.

Garrett received a patent for the traffic signal in 1923. The invention led to the development of a traffic system that improved safety enormously. The rights to the invention were sold to the General Electric Corporation for $40,000.

Garrett was also concerned about the plight of his fellow African Americans. He founded a newspaper, the *Cleveland Call*, to serve as a voice of the African-American community. He also ran for the city council in Cleveland.

Garrett's two important inventions, the gas mask and the traffic signal, are displayed at the Museum of African American History in Detroit, Michigan.

RILLIEUX, NORBERT
MECHANICAL ENGINEER

1806—1894
Birthplace: New Orleans, LA

Norbert Rillieux's invention had worldwide significance. In 1843, he developed a method for refining sugar. It consisted of a series of vacuum pans combined in a step-by-step process to turn heated, evaporated sugar into crystallized granules. Prior to Norbert's invention, sugar was an expensive item that was used only on special occasions. The old process used to make sugar was slow, dangerous and costly. Workers, usually slaves, stood over open, boiling kettles, using ladles to move sugarcane juice from one container to another. Many workers were injured by the hot, boiling liquid; some were even killed. The sugar that resulted from this dangerous process was dark and sticky and looked more like caramel than the sugar we use today.

Today, the process Rillieux invented is used throughout the sugar industry as well as in the manufacture of condensed milk, soap, gelatin, glue and other products.

Norbert was born on his father's plantation near New Orleans, Louisiana. His father was a wealthy French engineer, and his mother was a slave on the plantation. Children born of a union between a slave master and a slave were usually considered slaves, too. But Norbert was a free man, and his father even filed his birth with the city of New Orleans, listing himself as father.

Norbert's father sent Norbert to school in France. Educational opportunities for Blacks in the United States, slave or free, were almost non-existent during the early 1800s. Norbert was a brilliant student. After graduating, he taught mechanical engineering at his school. He later returned to New Orleans and began work on the invention that would change the sugar industry. He received a patent in 1843 and, in 1846, he received a second patent that incorporated changes he had made to his invention.

During a 1853 yellow fever epidemic in New Orleans, Norbert developed a way to deal with the disease. He suggested draining the swamps, thereby depriving the disease-breeding mosquitoes of their feeding grounds. The New Orleans Sewage Department turned him away but future scientific research proved that Norbert's theory was correct. In 1854, perhaps tired of the treatment African Americans received in the United States, Norbert returned to France. In France, he continued inventing, patenting an improved process of heating liquids with their own liquids.

Norbert died in France in 1894.

WALKER, MADAME C.J.
HAIR PRODUCTS INVENTOR

1867—1919
Birthplace: Delta, LA

Madame C. J. Walker was born Sarah Breedlove, the daughter of former slaves. She married at the age of 14 and became Sarah McWilliams. When her husband died, Sarah moved to St. Louis, Missouri. There she became a washerwoman and attended school at night. During this time, Sarah's hair began to fall out, and nothing she tried would stop it.

One night she had a dream about a cure for her hair loss. That started her on a search to find a cure. She found the ingredients, mixed them together, and tried the mixture on her hair. The formula was a success. Sarah started selling her new product door to door and eventually expanded her business to Denver, Colorado. There, in 1905, she married a newspaperman named Charles Walker. She began calling herself Madame C. J. Walker, and has been known by that name ever since.

Madame Walker became famous for her hair-care products. She is best known for inventing the pressing comb and a conditioner for straightening hair. At that time, many Black women thought that having straight hair was more beautiful than having hair left in its natural state. Today, many different hairstyles have become acceptable, in part because of Madame Walker's role in setting a standard for Black beauty that has helped to raise the self-esteem of Black women.

In 1910, Madame Walker established a factory in Indianapolis where she employed 5,000 Black women. An active community leader, Madame Walker also gave thousands of dollars to Tuskegee Institute, the NAACP, and other Black organizations and charities. She also helped establish the Mary McLeod Bethune School in Daytona Beach, Florida now known as Bethune-Cookman University.

Using her determination and boundless energy, Madame C. J. Walker followed her dream and became America's first Black female millionaire. When she died in her New York mansion, she left an estate valued at $2 million.

WOODS, GRANVILLE T.
ELECTRICAL ENGINEER

1856—1910
Birthplace: Columbus, OH

G ranville Woods was one of the pioneers of the Industrial Revolution. During his career he patented nearly 200 inventions. Some people called him the "Black Edison," but the comparison was unnecessary. Granville earned his own place in history.

Granville was born in 1856, several years before the Civil War began. Because slavery was prohibited in Ohio, he was born free. When he was 10 years old, Granville quit school and went to work in a machine shop to help his family. When he was 16 he moved to Missouri and took a job as a fireman and engineer on the railroad. There he developed an interest in science and read all the books about science that he could get his hands on. When he moved to New York City, he found a job in a machine shop and went to school at night to learn about electricity. Later, he worked on a steamship for two years and visited many parts of the world.

Granville began his career as one of America's most talented inventors in 1884. His first invention helped steam boiler furnaces heat homes and buildings better. Later that year he invented a new telephone transmitter. In 1885, he patented the "Telegraphony," a device that combined the telegraph with the telephone. He sold the rights to the American Bell Telephone Company for a large sum of money. Granville's next invention allowed conductors and engineers on moving trains to send and receive messages for the first time.

On January 29, 1901, Granville received a patent for one of his greatest inventions, "the third rail." The third rail powered subway trains with an electrical current, replacing electric engines. Granville's third rail is still used today in subway systems around the world. Several devices Granville invented led to the development of the automatic air brake. He sold the rights to these creations to the Westinghouse Electric Company of New York.

Granville faced many difficulties during his career. He went to court many times to protect the rights to his inventions. Even Thomas Edison's company tried to claim the rights to one invention. Granville, however, proved his right in court. Edison offered this great inventor a job with his company, but Granville wanted to be his own boss. Few inventors have contributed more to the electrical industry than Granville T. Woods.

CHRONOLOGY

1500s   The British, Dutch, Spanish, and Portuguese begin trafficking African people in the brutal slave trade.

1660   The number of American slaves increases rapidly as the British gain control over much of the slave trade.

1731   **Benjamin Banneker is born.**

1770   Phillis Wheatley publishes her first poem, becoming the earliest known published African-American woman writer.

1775   Crispus Attucks, a Black man, becomes the first person to die in the Boston Massacre, one of the major events of the American Revolution.

1776   The Declaration of Independence is signed, making the 13 colonies an independent nation.

1787   The African Free School, the first free secular school in New York City, opens.

        The Free African Society of Philadelphia, organized by Richard Allen and Absalom Jones, is formed.

1790   **The First United States Patent Act is enacted.**

1791   Toussaint L'Ouverture leads a successful slave revolt in Haiti. Haiti becomes the first independent Black nation in the Western Hemisphere.

1792   **Benjamin Banneker becomes the first African American to publish an almanac.**

1806   The African Meeting House in Boston, Massachusetts, is the first major building in Boston constructed solely by African Americans.

1822   Denmark Vesey organizes a slave revolt in Charleston, South Carolina.

1827   *Freedom's Journal*, the first Black newspaper, is published.

1831   Nat Turner leads a slave rebellion in Southampton, Virginia

1839   Joseph Cinque and other captured Africans take over the slave ship *Amistad*, demanding to be returned to Africa. They are ultimately set free by a United States Supreme Court decision in 1841.

1843   Sojourner Truth starts her own protest campaign against slavery.

        Norbert Rillieux patents his vacuum evaporation system, which revolutionizes the sugar industry and food production in general.

1846   Harriet Tubman escapes slavery and begins conducting on the Underground Railroad.

1848   The right of women to vote is proposed for the first time by women's rights leaders Elizabeth Cady Stanton and Lucretia Mott.

1853 William Wells Brown becomes America's first African–American novelist when his book *Clotel, Or, The President's Daughter: A Narrative of Slave Life in the United States,* is published in England.

1857 In the Dred Scott Decision, the United States Supreme Court denies citizenship rights to Blacks.

1861 The Civil War begins between the North and the South.

1863 President Abraham Lincoln signs the Emancipation Proclamation granting freedom to slaves in the states that are at war against the Union.

1864 Rebecca Cole and Rebecca Lee are the first African-American women in the United States to receive medical degrees.

1865 The Civil War ends with a Union victory.

1867 Madame C. J. Walker (Sarah Breedlove) is born.

1868 John Mercer Langston founds and organizes the Law Department at Howard University.

Howard University Medical School is founded in Washington, D.C.

1870 Hiram M. Revels becomes the first African-American United States senator when he is elected by the state of Mississippi.

1872 P.B.S. Pinchback of Louisiana becomes the first African American to serve as governor of a state.

1878 Meharry Medical College is founded in Nashville, TN.

1881 Tuskegee Institute is founded.

1882 Lewis H. Latimer patents the first cost-efficient method of producing carbon filaments for electric lights.

1883 Jan Matzeliger patents the first successful shoe lasting machine.

1891 Ida B. Wells starts her crusade against the lynching of African Americans. She later helps to found the NAACP.

1893 Dr. Daniel Hale Williams becomes the first to person to perform a heart operation successfully.

1896 George Washington Carver accepts a position as professor at Tuskegee Institute.

Mary Church Terrell is elected president of the National Association of Colored Women.

In *Plessey v. Ferguson*, the United States Supreme Court upholds legal segregation.

1897 Andrew J. Beard patents a coupling device for railroad cars.

1899 Mary Eliza Mahoney is the first African-American woman to graduate from a professional White nursing school.

1903 Maggie Lena Walker establishes the St. Luke Penny Savings Bank, which becomes the St. Luke Bank and Trust Company. She becomes America's first Black woman bank president.

1904 Mary McLeod Bethune establishes a school now known as Bethune-Cookman University.

1908 Jack Johnson becomes the first African-American heavyweight champion when he knocks out Tommy Burns in the fourteenth round.

The National Association for Colored Graduate Nurses is founded.

1909 The NAACP is formed.

1910 **Madame C. J. Walker opens her own beauty care factory. She becomes America's first Black self-made millionaire.**

1911 The Universal Negro Improvement Association (UNIA) is formed by Marcus Garvey.

1914 World War I begins. The United States enters in 1917.

1919 **Jane C. Wright is born. Madame C. J. Walker dies.**

1920s The Nineteenth Amendment to the Constitution guarantees women the right to vote.

1922 **Bessie Coleman, the first Black American female pilot, performs her air show in Chicago.**

1923 **Garrett A. Morgan patents a three-way automatic traffic signal.**

1926 Negro History Week, now Black History Month, is begun by Carter G. Woodson.

1928 **The Edgecombe Sanitarium is established in Harlem by Dr. Wiley Wilson and associates.**

1935 The National Council of Negro Women is formed.

1936 Jesse Owens becomes the first athlete to win four gold medals at the Olympics.

1940 **Frederick McKinley Jones patents a practical refrigeration system for trucks and railroad cars.**

Dr. Charles Richard Drew is the first person to set up a blood bank. Dr. Drew found that blood plasma could be used in transfusions rather that whole blood.

1945 World War II ends.

1947 Jackie Robinson becomes the first African American to play Major League Baseball in the modern era when he joins the Brooklyn Dodgers.

1954 The United States Supreme Court rules in *Brown v. Board of Education of Topeka, Kansas*, that segregation is unconstitutional.

1957   Althea Gibson becomes the first African American to win a Wimbledon singles title.

1959   Lorraine Hansberry's play "A Raisin in the Sun" wins the New York Drama Critics Award.

1960   Wilma Rudolph becomes the first woman to win three gold medals in track in the Olympics.

1961   The Freedom Rides begin. Wide-spread civil rights activies and mass protests heighten in the United States.

1962   South African leader Nelson Mandela is imprisoned.

1963   A Birmingham, Alabama church is bombed, killing four Black children.

1964   The Civil Rights Act is passed.

1965   Malcolm X is assassinated.

1968   Arthur Ashe becomes the first African-American male to win a major tennis tournament when he captures the singles title at the United States Lawn Tennis Association Open Tournament.

1968   Dr. Martin Luther King, Jr. is assassinated.

1983   Guion Bluford, Jr. becomes the first African American to make a space flight.

1986   The space shuttle *Challenger* explodes on its way into outer space. Aboard were seven crew members, including Ronald McNair.

1988   Jesse Jackson becomes the first African Americans to mount a serious run for the presidency of the United States.

1990   Nelson Mandela is released from prison.

1992   Mae C. Jemison becomes the first African-American woman to make a space flight.

1993   Toni Morrison becomes the first African American to win the Nobel Prize in literature.
        Dr. Jocelyn Elders is sworn in as United States surgeon general.

1995   Shirley Ann Jackson becomes head of the Nuclear Regulatory Commission.

1998   Dr. Patricia Bath receives patents for laser method and apparatus for removing cataracs.

GLOSSARY OF TERMS

aerodynamics	the dynamics of gases, especially of the atmospheric forces exerted on moving objects
aeronautics	the science or art of flight
almanac	an annual publication containing calendars, weather and astronomical forecasts, and other information
anthropology	the study of the origin and physical, social and cultural development and behavior of humans
arthritis	inflammation of a joint or joints, especially as in rheumatoid arthritis
astronomy	the science that deals with materials of the universe beyond the earth's atmosphere
astronaut	a person trained to make rocket flights into outer space
astrophysics	the branch of astronomy which deals primarily with the physical properties of the universe
aviation	the operation of an aircraft
botany	the science of plants
biochemistry	the chemistry of biological processes and substances
biology	the science of living organisms and life processes
chemistry	the scientific study of the composition, structure, properties and reactions of matter
dynamics	the branch of physics that deals with force, energy and motion and the relationship between them
dermatology	the medical study of skin physiology and pathology
electricity	a property of certain fundamental particles of all matter, such as electrons (negative charges) and protons (positive charges) that have a force field associated with and that can be separated by an expenditure of energy
engineer	1) one trained or engaged in a branch of engineering 2) one who operates an engine, especially a locomotive
engineering	1) the application of scientific principles to practical ends 2) the design and construction of large scale or complex structures such as bridges, roads and tunnels
entomology	the scientific study of insects
geology	the science dealing with the origin, history and study of the earth
glaucoma	an eye disease characterized by abnormally high pressure within the eyeball and partial or complete loss of vision
immunology	the study of the immunity (resistance) to diseases
invent	to think up, devise or fabricate in the mind

laser	l(ight) a(mplification by) s(timulated) e(mission of) r(adiation); a devise containing a substance the majority of whose atoms or molecules can be put into an excited energy state, allowing the substance to emit coherent light of a precise wavelength in an intense, narrow beam
lunar	of or pertaining to the moon
matter	the substance of which any physical object is composed
mechanical	having to do with, or having skill in the use of, machinery or tools
medicine	the science and art of diagnosing, treating, curing and preventing diseases, relieving pain, and improving and preserving health
neurology	the scientific and medical study of the nervous system and its disorders
observatory	a place used for making observations of astronomical or other natural phenomena
ophthalmology	the medical field encompassing the functions, anatomy, pathology and treatment of the eye
pharmacology	the study of the preparation, qualities, and use of drugs
physician	a person who is legally qualified to practice medicine; doctor
physics	the science of matter and energy and the interaction between them
planetarium	1) an apparatus or model representing the planetary system 2) device that produces a representation of the heavens by use of a number of moving objects
psychotherapy	treatment of emotional or mental disorders by psychological methods
rheumatology	branch of medicine dealing with the study and treatment of rheumatic diseases, characterized by pain and stiffness in the joints
satellite	1) a natural body that revolves around a planet 2) device designated to be launched into orbit around a planet
science	systematized knowledge derived from observation, study and experimentation carried on in order to determine the nature or principles of what is being studied
sickle-cell anemia	a hereditary disease marked by abnormal crescent-shaped red blood cells that are deficient in oxygen
spectograph	an optical device used to photograph or otherwise produce a representation of a spectrum
surveyor	one who inspects or studies land to determine position, boundaries, area, elevation and other factors by measuring angles and distances
zoologist	the biological science that deals with animals and animal life

SELECTED BIBLIOGRAPHY

Haber, Louis. *Black Pioneers of Science and Inventions*. San Diego: Harcourt Brace Jovanovich, 1987.

Hayden, Robert C. *Seven African-American Scientists*. Frederick, MD: Twenty-First Century Books, 1970.

Hudson, Wade and Valerie Wilson Wesley. *AFRO-BETS™ Book of Black Heroes From A to Z*. East Orange, NJ: Just Us Books, Inc., 1988.

McKissack, Patricia, and Frederick. *African-American Inventors*. Brookfield, CT: The Millbrook Press, 1994.

Ploski, Harry A. and James Williams. *The Negro Almanac, A Reference Work on the African American*. Detroit, MI: Gale Research Inc., 1989.

Sammons, Vivian Ovelton. *Blacks in Science and Medicine*. New York, NY: Hemisphere Publishing Corporation, 1990.

Sullivan, Otha Richard. *Black Stars, African-American Inventors*. New York, NY: John Wiley & Sons, Inc., 1998.

Sullivan, Otha Richard. *Black Stars, African-American Women: Scientists & Inventors*. New York, NY: John Wiley & Sons, Inc., 2002.

Turner, Glennette Tilley. *Lewis Howard Latimer*. Englewood Cliffs, NJ: Silver Burdett Press, Inc., a division of Simon and Schuster, 1991.

INDEX

ACKNOWLEDGEMENTS

PHOTO CREDITS
The photographs and illustrations reproduced in this book were obtained and used with permission from the sources listed below. Every effort has been made to trace ownership of all copyrighted materials and to secure the necessary permission to reprint each selection. In the event of any question regarding the fair use of any material, or any inadvertent error, the publisher will be happy to make the necessary correction in future printings.

Cover photos counterclockwise, left to right: Benjamin Banneker and Percy Julian, Photo and Prints Division, Schomburg Center for Research in Black Culture; Dr. Mae Jemison, NASA; Jocelyn Elders, Office of the Surgeon General; George Washington Carver, Art Resource Center; Mary Mahoney, Photo and Prints Division, Schomburg Center for Research in Black Culture; Dr. Hayes E. Willis, courtesy of the Willis family; Shirley Ann Jackson, Nuclear Regulatory Commission; Dr. Ben Carson, courtesy of Ben Carson; Ernest Just and Dr. Susan McKinley Stewart, Spingarn/Moorland Library, Howard University; center photo: Dr. Charles Drew and associates.

Interior photos: NASA: 10, 12, 13, 21, 25; Photo and Prints Division, Schomburg Center for Research in Black Culture: 11, 19, 22, 33, 35, 37, 38, 42, 47, 48, 53, 56, 58; Art Resource: 14; California State University: 15; Emory University: 16; AP World Wide Photos: 18; illustrations by Ron Garnett: 19, 26, 31, 44, 47, 50, 52; courtesy Shirley Ann Jackson: 20; Spingarn/Moorland Library, Howard University: 23, 41, 49, 51; National Science Foundation: 24; Library, American Museum of Natural History: 27; Jeffrey John Fearing: 29; *Leslie's Illustrated Weekly*: 32; Dr. Ben Carson: 30; Office of the Surgeon General: 34; National Library of Medicine, National Institutes of Health: 40; Planned Parenthood: 43; courtesy of the family of Dr. Hayes Emil Willis: 45; Lynn Museum: 54; illustrations by Howard Simpson: 55, 57, 59.

ABOUT THE AUTHOR

Wade Hudson has written and edited many books for young people. *AFRO-BETS*™ *Book of Black Heroes from A to Z; Jamal's Busy Day; Pass It On: African American Poetry for Children; How Sweet the Sound: African American Songs for Children; Anthony's Big Surprise; Great Black Heroes: Five Notable Inventors;* and *In Praise of Our Fathers and Our Mothers* are a few of his published titles. Mr. Hudson is also president of Just Us Books, Inc., a company he co-founded with his wife Cheryl. He lives in East Orange, NJ.